Israel at the Crossroads

ISRAEL
AT THE
CROSSROADS

by

ELIEZER SCHWEID

translated from the Hebrew

by

ALTON MEYER WINTERS

The Jewish Publication Society of America
PHILADELPHIA
5733 ▪ 1973

English translation copyright © 1973
By the Jewish Publication Society of America
All rights reserved
Originally published in Hebrew
by S. Zack & Co.,
Jerusalem, 1969
ISBN 0–8276–0001–1
Library of Congress catalog card number 72–87911
Manufactured in the United States of America
Designed by Sol Calvin Cohen

🌿 THE TRANSLATION OF THIS BOOK
INTO ENGLISH WAS MADE POSSIBLE THROUGH
A GRANT FROM THE ADOLF AMRAM FUND

iv

CONTENTS

PREFACE

to the English Translation

The pieces included in this collection were originally published in various periodicals. Readers desiring to refer to the Hebrew sources should see note 1, page 7, of the printed Hebrew text. Some of these articles were written before the Six-Day War, some after it. But they have all been thoroughly edited. They are all concerned with problems that were continually real or became so after the war. They dwell mainly on the question of our adherence to Judaism as culture, way of life, faith, and national unifier. It seems to me that there is value in publishing these essays in collected form at present. In this manner they complement one another and comprise a single fabric. Thus they may contribute something to the clarification of those problems which we are forced to face.

It goes without saying that I have published only those articles which express my present views. The single exception is "Zionism under Testing," which voices the climate of opinion that preceded the Six-Day War. I no longer identify with a portion of what is stated there. But I decided to include it in this collection because a part of its material still seems correct and relevant to me. Furthermore, making plain the change that has occurred in my evaluation from one period to the next is in and of itself relevant to our issue. At any rate, in order to prevent misunderstanding, I have added notes stating my present reservations.

Finally, I see a need to build fences against the misunderstanding which "A Time of Returning" might stir. When it was first published it aroused a tempestuous debate which proceeded, at least in part, from a lack of comprehension which was, it seems to me, the result of excessive political emotionalism. I wish to emphasize, therefore, that it is not a political piece but a reflection on personal experience, though I think it has public applications. It should be examined first of all from this point of view. I desire, therefore, to direct the attention of the reader to the rejoinders to two opponents, Amos Oz and Pinchas Rosenblüt. Such is not my usual practice (for one normally presents the actual statements of the opponents). But the emotionalism has not abated, and there exists the possibility that additional misunderstanding will be created. It is my hope that by avoiding irrelevant debate, the discussion stimulated by this collection will be directed into the proper channel.

Furthermore, in the four years that have passed since the original Hebrew publication of this book, many changes have taken place in the political and social reality of the State of Israel. It is only natural that these changes have affected my estimate and views of the situation. This applies particularly to "A Time of Returning." The reader will understand that piece better perhaps if he keeps in mind the fact that it was composed just a few months after the Six-Day War. The essay shows signs of emotionalism which certainly do not add to its clarity and consistency. If I were to write it now, it would be fundamentally different in both content and style. If justification must be offered for the present appearance of this essay in English, it may be said that it offers testimony on the power of an experience which brought about a distinct alteration in my views and which still forms the background of my activity. At the same time, I must emphasize that I have come quite some distance from several parts of that essay. I fear that it will not be correctly understood by readers who did not share directly in the experience. It is for that reason that I have made several changes and deletions in the piece and have also given it a different place in the order of chapters from that which it occupied in the original. Placed between the two articles on the meaning of Zionism, this essay may be more understandable. In its position in this volume, it may also clarify the change that has occurred in my approaches to Zionism before and after the Six-Day War.

E. S.

TO MY DAUGHTER MICHAL

Israel at the Crossroads

1

AT THE BREAKING POINT

The Six-Day War exposed once again, and in dramatic fashion, a whole range of problems to which Israeli Jewry has been subject since the establishment of the State. These include the tension of relationships between Israel and the Arabs, as well as between Israel and the other countries involved—directly or indirectly—in the dispute; the tension of relationships between religious and secular elements within Israel, and fundamentally the problem which seems to me to be the most important and basic of them all: the tension in the spiritual life of every thinking person, be he religious or not, who is caught somewhere between the polar extremities on the question of his national and cultural identification as a Jew. This is, first of all, a question of his acceptance or rejection of the very fact of his position within this destiny and this culture. Then it is a question of his being able to find the fulfillment of his intellectual life and the substance of his existence in this culture.

One can employ a simplistic approach to each of these questions, laying bare an unequivocal process— positive or negative—in the political, cultural, or social reality through which we are living. Immediately following the victory in the Six-Day War there was a dominant feeling among us that from then on we were

3

surely close to peace with the Arab nations. We thought that the reawakening in the Jewish communities abroad bore witness that the Jews living there had uncompromisingly displayed their identification with the State of Israel and that they were ready to give active expression to that identification. It seemed to us that the barriers of reserve and hostility between the religionists and secularists in Israel had been breached and that both sides had declared that they had one fate and were of one heart. And we believed that even Jews who were very distant from an awareness of belonging to Jewish history and its heritage had rediscovered their place within it.

Today, in contrast, the more we move away from the flood of feelings of the moment of victory, the more we become inclined toward the opposite evaluation; this is a reversion to the position we held before the Six-Day War. The dispute between Israel and the Arab states appears to us to be one from which there is no escape to a stable peace. The Diaspora communities appear to be immersed in a rapid and irreversible process of assimilation into their environments, from both the national and the cultural points of view. The rift between religionists and secularists seems to be expanding and to be near the breaking point. The danger that the religious Jew will lose his attachment to the people of Israel, while the secular Jew will lose his sense of adherence to the cultural heritage of Judaism, has begun to look like a near certainty.

Whether the words are uttered or the dread secret is kept locked in the heart, we are confronted with the bitter prospect of total collapse. But because both evaluations have bases in fact, it is correct to state that neither of them by itself can encompass the whole

4

truth. We find ourselves in the very throes of a process which is ambiguous and ambivalent at every single level. It contains both the propulsion toward the extremes and the attraction toward the center; thus in and of itself it still offers no decisive force. The importance of the shock we felt during the Six-Day War was first and foremost that it exposed this ambiguity by laying bare with absolute clarity both the risk and the opportunity in our situation. It also reinforced both of them in an extreme manner.

The opportunity rests, of course, in the very fact of our presence in the entirety of the land of Israel. That signifies the dominance of our political and military weight in the Middle East, the enhancement of our security situation, the revival of the potentiality for immigration and settlement, and the realization of the Zionist vision in its full original sense and compass: the return of the Jewish people to the land of its fathers. The opportunity rests also in the possibility of permanently tying the Jews of the world to Israel as a Diaspora which supplies immigration and builds, directly with us, the homeland of the entire Jewish people. The opportunity lies in identification with the people, with what happens to the people, and with the people's heritage. It is an opportunity to mend the spiritual rift that divides us and to reestablish the conditions whereby every Jew draws sustenance from the sources of Judaism.

However, the danger is no less terrifying. It is that peril which lies in the worsening and the perpetualization of hostility between the Arabs and ourselves and, against that background, between us and the East European powers, as well as a portion of the West. It is a danger which rests in the position of a slight majority over a large minority, and of a conquering majority over a subdued minority. That situation implies an increasing tendency toward militarism and chauvinism, as well as the conversion of our lives into a function of a savage war of survival. This situation entails the risk of moral and cultural impoverishment, inner despair, and alienation between Israel and world Jewry, and between the thinking Jew and his heritage.

Both evaluations are based on the same set of facts, which we are directly experiencing. They rise up before us as the peril or the potential *between which we are called upon to decide* through deeds that we can perform by our own free choice.

Being a Jew is a fact of one's destiny with which a person should reconcile himself by conscious choice. One is born to Judaism; but until he chooses it as a way of life and a philosophy, it is not completed within him. He lives his Jewish life with a divided heart. The aspiration for "normalization" of the life of the Jewish people in modern times, whether by way of assimilation among the nations or through the establishment of a Jewish state, expressed a weariness with that burden. It expressed the lack of will to make the choice. But even unwillingness to choose is an act of choice, positive or negative. The constructive character of Zionism was just another expression of that same condition. It was a confirmation on the basis of a protest against the fact of Jewish identification, a protest that was made as a conscious choice. The State of Israel did not rise out of external historical processes, though certain causes made it possible. It arose because the Zionist movement willed it. The continuation of the existence of the State is thus dependent on the perpetuation of the will for its survival. It is true that we sank into an atrophy of the will following the War of Independence. Perhaps this was due to the achievement and to the fatigue resulting from the effort it demanded. Or perhaps it was because it seemed to us that things no longer depended on the will of individuals or even on the collective will, that there was no longer any choice to be made.

Be that as it may, we expected to accept our own independence and unity as matters of course, and thus we risked the loss of everything we had gained. The Six-Day War once again brought us into confrontation with the potential and the peril, and once more forced us to make a choice. This was, without a doubt, an arrival at a point of crisis.

It was crisis in the usual meaning of the word in our day: a condition of extreme upset. And it was crisis in the original biblical meaning of the Hebrew expression *ad mashber*, signifying a situation on the threshold of hope (as in Isaiah 37:3, where the phrase is generally translated "to the birth"). If we openly confront the potentials and the perils, we shall choose hope. If we ignore those choices, we shall opt for upheaval. One way or the other, the responsibility for better or worse will fall first and foremost on us. Therefore, we must once again will—to choose.

2
WHAT DOES IT MEAN
TO BE A JEW?

I

Researchers in the subject of modern Jewish history have pointed out that, in a way not true of earlier periods, the Jewish individual and the Jewish community in modern times have been occupied with the problem of identification. Of course, in both antiquity and in the Middle Ages, affiliation with Jewry and Judaism was never a cut-and-dried thing to be taken for granted. Even then the Jew was required to choose Judaism willingly as a way of life and to confess it as a revealed religion. Even then he was required to testify to his election by his deeds, his whole manner of living, and—in times of trial—his willingness to undergo martyrdom.

But until the end of Middle Ages the question of who is a Jew never came up outside of Jewish religious law. And the answer given on that plane was, in any case, clear and unwavering. Nor did the question of *what* is a Jew come out until the end of medieval times. For despite the various conflicting views found within the framework of the Jewish religion, the authority of scripture and halakhah to shape the Jew's way of life was powerful and clear. In early modern times, with the emergence of the desire for political and social intermingling with the European environment—that is, when a great many individuals and entire communities began to cast off the yoke of Jewish law—the two questions came up simultaneously.

Not all Jews could agree on leaving the decision about their connection with Judaism and that of their children in the hands of the masters of halakhah. In any case, they were not prepared to define their Jewishness in terms of the traditional sources and in accord with the way of life that had been fashioned on the authority of those sources. Those Jews who had cast off the yoke of halakhah were unable to propound any independent stable framework to take its place. They came to regard their Jewish identity as a troublesome problem. Indeed, the very raising of the question was perhaps at times the only clear indication of their Jewishness. They started out by asking themselves to what extent they were Jewish. That meant asking whether the fact of their being Jews defined their roles in all areas of political, social, and cultural activity—or only in a part of those areas, leaving Jews no different from others for the remainder.

However, the question automatically came up as to the quality of the difference even in those areas where such difference was assumed and actually existed. What caused it? What defined it? What justified it? To use terms that were dear to the heart of European Jewry in the last generation, why should we wish to hold on to our Jewishness? Because it is obvious that partial adherence to Judaism weakens the content embraced by the totality and demanding total commitment, no less than it stunts the reach of Judaism. Yet those Jews who cast off the yoke of Jewish law still had an honest desire to preserve their Jewish identity. That was the root of the problem.

What has been said so far has intentionally been kept in general terms. Those "modern times" are no longer so modern. They saw many changes and can be divided into their own "antiquity" and "middle ages" and "modernity." Even the question of Jewish identity passed through many transformations during that period. There were changes in both its formulation and the answers given to it. We do not intend to trace all those transformations. The general background was drawn simply to serve as a backdrop for the change brought about by the State of Israel in the very formulation of the question. We shall see how the existence of the of the State has made invalid several of the answers that used to be acceptable—and still are among large sections of the Jewish public.

Zionism proposed a Jewish state as a solution to both the Jewish problem and the problem of Judaism. The State apparently redefined an all-inclusive structure of Jewish life. This structure supposedly offered unity in the social, political, and cultural spheres. By adherence to this State, each Jew was to be able to give his Jewishness an all-embracing and secure definition, just as it was during ancient and medieval times. At least within the State, that dualism of belonging to a Jewish life structure and a surrounding non-Jewish world at the same time was no longer to exist. Apparently, the question of Jewish identity would not have to be asked in the State of Israel. It was solved. Except that the solution raised the question in a new form. Consider this: from the day the State was established until this moment, that question has never been off our agenda. It has been repeatedly discussed in all the arenas— among the political parties, among individuals in society, and in our intellectual life.

11

II

Today we encounter the question of what it means to be a Jew on three planes. The first plane concerns relations between Israel and the Diaspora. It is vital for both the preservation of the State of Israel and the survival of the Diaspora that the tie between them be perpetuated. However, the clear and simple definition of Jewish identity within the confines of the State has very much broadened the difference between the Jewish community residing in Israel and Jews abroad. Jews in the Diaspora aspire to cultural, political, and social assimilation in the European or American environment. Alienation of language, culture, and lifestyle and awareness of political and social affiliation are, more and more, becoming a reality between Israel and the Diaspora. The political-national Jewishness of the Israeli is, therefore, a divisive rather than a cohesive factor.

Indeed, it appears that this description of the problem is not to be shaken at several principal points. Still, there is room to revise and deepen it further. One assumption, which is swallowed up among the words as if it were obvious, should be examined more closely. That is the assumption that the relationship of Israel to the Diaspora is one between a community whose adherence to Jewishness is clear and sure, and a group whose Jewish affiliation is weak and vague. Most of the solutions for this problem suggested with Zionist circles are based on this simplistic assumption.

However, the reality in the State of Israel and in the Diaspora is much more complex. On one hand, the process of drifting away from the special character of Jewish life and culture is also going on in the State of Israel; on the other, the desire for the preservation

12

of something of Jewish content is no less powerful in the Golah than it is in Israel. In this respect, there exists a parallel between Israel and the Diaspora, and that creates an opening for mutual understanding between them. But it also appears that the drifting away from the special Jewish life-style is not the same in Israel as that process is abroad. Still worse, the focal point of identification with the Jewish life structure is not the same in the two communities. In Israel, there is a growing tendency to define Jewishness in terms of society and state. From this point of view, the demand of Jewish identity is structural and all-embracing. In respect to his consciousness of national, political, and social affiliation the Jew must be *all* Jew and *only* Jew. But it is precisely this tendency which is alien to most Jews abroad. For, despite their sympathy for the State of Israel and their acceptance of the importance of its survival from their own point of view, they consider themselves citizens and nationals of their countries of residence.

In the Diaspora there is an increasing tendency to define Jewishness in terms of a religious philosophy and a traditional way of life. From this point of view, the need for Jewish identification is spiritual and not total. This Jew must preserve his unique character within an open society and take an active part in the whole fabric of its cultural and social creativity. But this is a tendency which is exactly alien to most of the Jews of Israel. From the point of view of their philosophy and life-style, they are far removed from religion and tradition. At the same time, their activity is carried on within a closed Jewish society. This fundamental difference between the focal points of Jewish identification in the State of Israel and in the Diaspora is a source of many misunderstandings and frustrations. The Israeli expects deeds, feelings, and thoughts for which the Jew in the Diaspora has not the slightest inclination. And Jews overseas demand that Israel be something for them which it just cannot be.

We shall not go so far as to say that these expectations are altogether unfulfilled. They are partially fulfilled. Perhaps it is correct to state that they are fulfilled in a peripheral manner. This is so because there is a close theoretical connection between the political-national definition of Jewishness and its definition as a religion and traditional way of life. These two definitions depend upon one another at their bases, and we shall have more to say about that later. This is why mutual frustration does not cause an abandonment of hope and demanding from either of the two sides. Thus the tie persists. But there is no ignoring the process of alienation and the threatening danger of schism. It is these perils which drive us to ask: What is the common denominator between Israel and world Jewry? What can guarantee the tie for the future? What does it mean to be a Jew?

The second plane on which we meet the problem is that of the relations among sections of the Jewish community in the State of Israel itself. At this point, we must delimit our previous statements. Only by generalization and simplification can one present the State of Israel and the Diaspora as if they were two communities, each definable in a given situation and position. Practically speaking, neither world Jewry nor Israeli Jewry is of one piece. Therefore, the question of a common denominator between the political-national approach and the religious approach, even

14

with different emphases, exists not just between them but also within each of them. What is the connection between the religious sections called Orthodox, and the non-Orthodox elements in Jewish society? This problem is more serious in Israel than in the Diaspora. That is not just because Orthodoxy is generally less fanatic in the Golah. Nor is it simply because the non-Orthodox are inclined to define themselves, out of a positive relationship to religion and tradition, as liberal religionists. In Israel, Orthodoxy is more fanatical and domineering, while the non-Orthodox tend to label themselves—on the basis of indifference or even negativism toward religion and tradition—as secularists. More decisive than any of the foregoing, however, is the fact that in a Jewish society that is independent from the political standpoint, the tendency toward polarization is encouraged. So the differences find expression in direct and extreme clashes.

In respect to internal relations, the clearly political structure is far from assuring unity. On the contrary, it exacerbates fragmentation. The question may be asked as to how long that structure will be able to survive without a more substantial basis for cooperation among the parts of the community which it encompasses. But we would be off the mark if we described the tendency toward polarization between the Orthodox and the secular communities in Israel as a result of the difference between those who have remained faithful to the authentic Jewish tradition and those who are in a process of drifting away from it in alienation. Even here, the gravity of the problem consists in the fact that the two communities have grown distant, in different directions and from different points of view, from that original heritage which

15

knew no division between Judaism as a nation and culture as contrasted with a Judaism of faith and religious law. But the two communities have remained faithful to their Jewish identity, though they have defined it around two different centers of focus—faith and halakhah on one side, nation and culture on the other.

This is the background of the misunderstanding between these two communities. This is the background of the expectations that are never fulfilled, the demands that are not answered, and the mutual frustration that finds its voice in some political and social free-for-alls.

To repeat, we would be exaggerating if we said that the frustration is absolute. There are situations where the expectations are encouraged and even answered, showing results in the reality of the day-to-day life of the State. Here, too, we can say that this is because there is a theoretical tie, cultural-historic as well as halakhic, between the national and the religious definitions of Judaism. For this reason, the two opposing sides can neither give one another up nor give in to one another.

But there is no ignoring the process of polarization and the danger of the ultimate rift it might bring. These conditions, then, also drive us to ask: What is the common denominator between the communal segments of Israel? What can assure their tie in the future? What does it mean to be a Jew?

The third plane on which we encounter the problem is that of the inner difficulties in the heart and mind of the contemporary Jew. In this case, too, we must first specify a generalization in broader terms than in our earlier remarks. Only in a schematically simplistic fashion is it possible to place the Orthodox community in Israel over against the secular as two groups, each of which is defined in a given situation and a certain position. In practice, it is not just that the Orthodox group is not of one piece or that the secular group is not either; in every one of the intermediate shadings and in the mind of every thinking person you find unrest and hesitation between the two pathways. It appears that only organizational structures represent the conflicting tendencies which exist in the heart of individuals as clearly crystallized positions. In practice, polarization reveals itself as a tragic background from within. For the Jew who labels himself Orthodox cannot free himself from emotional and intellectual attachment to the Jewish people in general, and the secular Jew cannot free himself from the emotional and intellectual tug of the religious tradition. He is also frequently driven to inquire what his being Jewish "gives" him. Is it a fact of fate with which he must make his peace? Is it something he must delve into for cultural fulfillment with which to shape his life beyond the boundary of his national identification? Or does it offer a spiritual heritage with which he can identify and which he can use to fashion his way of life, his sensations, and his philosophy with integrity?

It is obvious that these questions do not come up in the mind of a Jew living in Israel as the problem of accepting or rejecting a life within the framework of a Jewish community. In a closed society such a question is ruled out from the start. But that does not at all diminish the severity of the problem. First, the State of Israel was created out of a revolt against the fate of the Jewish people in the Exile, as well as because of a

17

wish for normalization of relations with its surroundings. But also within the State—or particularly within it—the abnormal destiny of the Jewish people took on prominence because of the extreme tension that was created between the State and its surroundings. The Jew living in Israel is exposed to the daily test of mortal fear and to demands for loyalty and sacrifice. Even if he sees no chance of being rescued from the bonds of his Jewish fate or of avoiding its consequences as an individual, therefore, it is impossible that there should not stir within him, sooner or later, the question of his inner willingness to be reconciled with that fate or to find meaning in it.

Does separate Jewish existence offer something that can make sense of the cruel test to which it submits us?

Second, the State of Israel was created not only out of revolt against the destiny of the Jewish people in the Diaspora, but also with a mind to cutting loose from the tradition and its values as they had been shaped in the Exile. If for no other reason than that, the consciousness of the empty cultural space grew ever more powerful among the Jewish community that was coming into being in the land of Israel. When the process of national political construction attained its great success, there immediately arose the question of the cultural content for whose perpetuation and continuity such a tremendous effort had been expended. Does the Jewish heritage, then, contain enough to satisfy the complex of spiritual needs of the Jewish community in Israel? Does it offer something with which to answer the complex of questions asked by the individual as human being? Or perhaps the geometrical center of national identification of the secular Jew is not congruent with the center of his life as a man of culture. The national tie of the secular Jew drives him to search for solutions within the area of his traditional heritage. But because of that tie he suffers a feeling of alienation from that heritage. At one and the same time he drifts away and approaches closer. But he can never achieve fulfillment and unity in his cultural life.

It is proper to stress here that the integration of the life of the mind and the life of the spirit is not a problem just for the secular Jew. The advantage of the secular Jew is that for the most part he recognizes his problematic state, defines it, and tries to face up to it. The weakness of the extreme Orthodox Jew (even if this weakness gives the appearance of strength and firmness) is that he tends to hide from his problematic condition and is not prepared to confront it. However, it is a fact that in exacting adherence to the Torah and the commandments in the narrowest sense, there is embodied a withdrawal not only from the totality of the general culture of our era, but also from the cultural fullness within which Jewish tradition came into being. Furthermore, meticulous adherence to Torah and commandments in the most limited sense creates an ambiguous relationship of reluctance combined with dependence, or of opposition together with a condition of reliance in regard to the all-embracing framework of Jewish society and the Jewish State. Such a relationship does not facilitate the growth of full and independent social experience. And it cannot foster the development of a full spiritual creativity free of hindrance and distortion.

The polarity of relationships between the State of Israel and the Diaspora, as well as between the various sectors of the Israeli public, makes its appearance as

19

an inner background within the mind of every individual. This, it would seem, is the most profound background for the misunderstanding, the unrealized hopes, and the searchings that bring no results even in the shaping of personal life-styles or in the process of spiritual creativity.

It would be going too far to say that struggle never brings agreement or positive gain. Only at the fringes of each group do we find clearly sterile negation of tradition and heritage, on the one hand, and of the national structure and its political-social values, on the other. As a rule, every person is looking for a synthesis of some kind and putting it into practice within the framework of an ideological movement or a social group to which he feels close. For, as has been said, nationalism leads to the tradition, and the tradition leads to nationalism. But there is no longer any hiding from the worsening psychological rift, or from the danger of spiritual frustration and the impoverishment of the intellectual experience which that entails.

Of necessity, the questions arise here not in their national, or in their social or political, formulation; but rather in the serious and profound personal wording that takes precedence over all else. What are the values that, with integrity, can sustain and shape the lifestyle and the creativity of the contemporary Jew? What can provide an outlet for his aspiration to independent spiritual creativity and to a full and meaningful personal life? What then does it mean to be a Jew?

III

From what has been said so far, one may discern three main directions in which the literature of modern

Jewish thought has gone in search of an answer to the question of identification. There is the *religious* direction, for one, and the *national* direction; these are the two directions which we might describe schematically as the bifurcation of the original oneness of a religion-nation. That oneness was the outstanding mark of Jewish experience during antiquity and medieval times. And, in the middle area, there is the *cultural* direction which takes a position between the other two. Let us now reflect on these three directions and determine the relationship between them, so that we may understand what they have to tell us today.

Is it possible to derive a common denominator for all the various solutions that have been put forth from the religious direction? Anyone who examines the various views of the nature of the Jewish religion in the modern age, and especially the confusing mixture of religious tradition with cultural heritage that dominates so many of them, is going to have some serious doubts. Yet one can describe all these views as revolving, in narrower or wider circles, about one central point. That center is formulated in the simplistic extreme in the Orthodoxy of the *Agudat Israel* type: being a Jew means living by the commandments of the Torah as presented in the *Shulhan Arukh*, obeying the directives of the sages who have been ordained to determine the halakhah, and believing in the truth of everything that the Torah teaches according to the interpretation of scholars, whose greatness in halakhah also invests them with superiority in this area.

One must recognize the limitations of this definition, for it answers only the question of what it means to be a Jew and not who is a Jew. That last question is covered by the pithy, on-target reply of Rabbi E. S. Hartom: "A Jew is a person who, according to Jewish law, is obligated to observe the Torah." The emphasis there is on the word obligated; the person is a Jew in the eyes of the halakhah whether he fulfills his obligation or not. But there is a clear connection between this answer to the question of who is a Jew and the normative-halakhic answer on the problem of the nature of Judaism. Even someone who does not live within its framework is still considered a Jew by it. This is the starting point of the rigidity and extremism with which the masters of the religious direction cling to their halakhic definition, both in regard to the norm of the halakhah itself and in regard to the force of its obligatory nature. It is this which determines the attitude of closeness or distance which they show to those who do not live by Jewish law.

Let us place the poles side by side. According to the Reform interpretation, even one who does not live by the halakhah, as they define it, is still a Jew. In their view, one must also be tolerant of someone who is not religious at all, even of an apostate. In contrast, by the most extreme Orthodox interpretation, even someone who lives by the halakhah, but not according to their understanding of it—in fact, perhaps that person especially, as opposed to someone who is not at all religious and who is not involved in decisions of Jewish law—is a sinful Jew, and the apostate even more so.

Despite these differences, they share the common assumption that belief in a God who is revealed to Israel and a way of life to which one is obligated according to that belief define what being Jewish means. Anyone who does not live by this assumption, even if

22

he does not withdraw from his affiliation with Jewry, is not essentially a Jew.

The group taking the second direction, the national-political, also strives for a simple, unequivocal definition. It does so in spite of the multiplicity of views and the intermingling of categories between this direction and the cultural direction. Here we shall use the most extremely simplistic formulation, that of Jacob Klatzkin. Various factors may lead human beings to recognize themselves, and to be recognized by others, as members of a single nation. But nationality can be exhaustively defined as consciousness of unity against a background of common origin and common fate. All obligations to a certain faith, way of life, or culture are canceled out, therefore, in this definition. They can be either causes or effects. They cannot be part of the definition. According to this view, it is possible to admit that it was the religion which united the tribes of ancient Israel into a nation and preserved that unity afterwards. As a result of the religion, a national culture of a unique character came into being. It could also be confessed that, for the moment, the religious factor was still strong enough among certain elements of both the Jewish people and the European environment to prevent the complete assimilation of the Jews. That is, the fact that even the Jewish atheist is not a Christian and is alien to the Christian foundation of European culture separates and isolates him. That causes him to regard himself as a Jew by nationality. But it is clear that his attachment to Jewishness in this manner holds no religious content. Furthermore, it is clear that the influence which religion retains over the Jew in modern times is, by this view, a passing historical phase. In general, religion's time has passed. Its place is being taken over by a universal secular culture, and this is nothing more than a matter of historical process. Being a Jew therefore means being a person who regards himself, and is regarded by others, as a member of the Jewish nation.

Since the religious factor which gave rise to this consciousness is growing weaker and weaker, it is necessary, according to this viewpoint, to place Jewish peoplehood on a political basis. The Jews will not be able to preserve their Jewish identity in the Diaspora much longer. The burdensome isolation of the non-religious Jew from Christian society will continue only during the period of transition. Jewish survival is impossible even temporarily except on the basis of hope for a state. And when the process of evolution of the secular culture has borne its fruit, Jewish peoplehood will survive only within the borders of the Jewish State.

Of course, this definition of the nature of Jewishness has an effect on the answer to the problem of who is a Jew—because the rejection of the religious basis in the national definition greatly broadens (at least theoretically) the entire structure. A Jew is anyone who looks upon himself as a Jew and takes part in Jewish life, as defined above on a social-political basis. The question of whether he observes the halakhah or is obligated to do so is, from this point of view, completely off the subject. Yet it must be pointed out that in practice a gap was created between this simple definition of Jewishness and its application to individuals. The Jewish community's acceptance of an individual's statement that he is a Jew by nationality does not derive from this definition of nationhood. It

24

derives rather from the causes that lead to the individual's statement. That is, it depends upon certain conditions under which the community regards this individual as a member participating in its totality. From this point of view, for example, the question of the identity of an apostate would be more serious for a national Jew than for a religious Jew. This means that even in this area we can find various, and even conflicting, positions—all in keeping with the degree of extremism and simplification of their understanding of the formula of "consciousness of unity" against the background of common origin.

Rejection of the concept of assimilation of the Diaspora, dissatisfaction with the superficial structure of political unity, lack of faith in the ability of a political structure to preserve itself without strong inner support—all these feelings are likely to lead to a reassignment of greater importance to the spiritual factor, if only as a means to an end. In other words, the nationalistic definition of Jewish identity must lead to a search for a common denominator, beyond nationality, to serve as its own base. Nevertheless, common to all the views that derive from the national definition is the assumption that, at least to start with, an attachment to Jewishness does not entail faith, philosophy, or way of life—only Jewish birth, a sense of belonging, and loyalty to the unified community through consciousness of a shared destiny. Anyone included in this framework, even if he takes no part in the spiritual heritage of past generations of his people, is called a Jew.

The third direction, as we have said, makes its way between the other two. We come to it from the religious direction when it dawns on us that the religion itself, whether defined as faith or halakhah, is unable to survive except through the medium of a social carrier whose role is more than religious. We approach it from the national direction when we come to realize that the sense of belonging is transmitted and sustained only by a social carrier whose role is more than national. From both directions, one may arrive at the paradoxical conclusion that Judaism cannot survive in its definitions as either faith or folk unless it contains something more than religion or peoplehood. That is, it must also be a culture, including the creative work of Jews in every area of human life.

Yet it must be emphasized that the tendency toward the cultural definition is stronger and clearer in the nationalist direction and weaker and more blurred in the religious. Why should this be? The reason would seem to be that, while the religious definition is caught up in content, the nationalist definition of Jewishness works with a structure that is devoid of values. The nationalists are, therefore, more sensitive to their lack. A further reason is that from the religious point of view one can look upon Jewish culture as an effect which has indubitably flowed from faith and is defined by religion, and not as something which gives a definition to the religion itself.

Thus we find that most of the streams of modern Jewish nationalist thought have also arrived, directly or indirectly, at a cultural definition of Jewishness. Ahad Ha-am's doctrine is an outstanding example. Jewishness is for him first and foremost a national framework, the base of which lies in a biologic sense of belonging. The Jew, like a member of any other people, is born to Jewishness. He does not choose it. In his own will to survive, he embodies the entire people's will to survive. All the sense of obligation for faith, way of life, or culture seems to be absent here. But one who reflects deeply will realize that placing nationalism on the foundation of a sense of belonging which is biologically inherited is intended not only to give it prime force, but also to enrich it with all the values by which man's creative activity is embodied. The whole personality thus enters the framework of national life, to the point where the survival of the group takes precedence over that of the individual.

How so? Ahad Ha-am asserts that all of a nation's creative works express its struggle for survival under constantly changing conditions throughout its history. He states that without past memory and future hope —two factors which balance one another—continuity would cease in both the life of the individual and that of the people. Destruction would follow. This means that attachment to the past is a vital demand of the national will to survive, to the point where the religion will be defined even for the nonreligious Jew as a cultural possession which he is obliged to retain. This obligation certainly cannot be preserved except through a choice of contents, or through their reinterpretation beyond their simple meaning. Ahad Ha-am, of course, made many experiments with this view in mind. From his standpoint, however, the demand to give attention to religious content was important in and of itself. He felt that it was not even required to use content directly to define a philosophy or fashion a way of life; the content could simply be a part of the cultural memory.

In other words, a Jew must study Bible, Mishnah, and Talmud. He has to accept certain fundamentals of

Jewish tradition, even if he is not religious—because the Jew was preserved by these things in the past, and he cannot survive in the future without them. A Jew must find a synthesis between his philosophy and way of life as they have been influenced by his European surroundings and the heritage of Jewish culture. For without such a synthesis, he will be unable to lead a full personal life within the framework of the Jewish community. He would thus deprive both himself and his people of something valuable.

Ahad Ha-am's doctrine, on the whole, was an effort to stir the Jewish intelligentsia to search for a synthesis that would save the Jewish people from destruction. The same is true of the teaching of A. D. Gordon, despite the fact that Gordon's basis in theory and experience was quite far from that of Ahad Ha-am. Gordon did not attribute primary importance to the bequeathal of the cultural heritage from generation to generation. For him, this was a necessary but marginal factor. Instead, he greatly expanded the basis of the national collective. This was no longer a biologic sense of belonging anchored in the will for survival. It became, for Gordon, a cosmic creative force possessed of its own outstanding qualities. This force was embodied anew in the creative acts of the people from generation to generation. But since it was the same creative force, the relationship and continuity among all its works was recognizable from the start. What is more, according to this view, membership in the nation embraced the whole abundance of a person's creativity in all areas of his life. Gordon is nationalist in content, not in structure.

Y. Kaufmann is far removed in his theoretical basis from both Ahad Ha-am and A. D. Gordon; he is close to the nationalist definition of Jacob Klatzkin. Kaufmann does more than value the Jewish religion as the main, if not the only, factor in the formation and preservation of nationalism in the past. He also specifies the need to base this nationalism in the future on both a political structure and a Hebrew culture which will remain open to past Jewish creativity throughout its entire compass.

In such views, then, a tendency emerges to seek content that will justify the preservation of the form. From this, it is not far to the assumption that the national structure in and of itself has no importance when all is said and done. For it is nothing more than a condition for the maintenance of contents with which the Jew identifies and from which he continues to create—though he is not obligated to them as an Orthodox Jew is obligated to the tenets of faith or the commandments of halakhah. By this formulation, then, it is possible to establish the cultural definition as an independent direction. Such is the case despite the fact that when we try to determine which are those special values possessed by Judaism as a culture and which are its outstanding features, we confront a problem which we may not be able to master. Judaism as a culture, cut off from its religious foundation, is not subject to definition.

An examination of these three directions, therefore, establishes that they are not clearly distinguishable from one another. Rather, they touch and create intermediate shadings by their combinations. A person who holds on to the Jewish religion necessarily takes possession of the culture which has accumulated around the tradition and its institutions and its ritual throughout the generations. He selects from it what is suitable for himself. He automatically affiliates himself with the Jewish nationality, because the Jewish religion is by nature a national religion. One who defines his Jewishness as "only" a nationality is led—in greater or lesser measure, according to his inclination and education—to accept something of Jewish culture. And since Jewish culture has a firm connection with the religion, through it he comes to cement a tie with religious values, if only in terms of criticism or modernist interpretation. This applies all the more to one who defines his Jewishness directly as a cultural attachment. His view necessitates an effort to bridge the gap between the nationalist and the religious definitions by understanding the cultural definition as embracing its two predecessors. However, this description of the connection between the various directions, though fundamentally correct, is rather simplistic.

A look at reality instructs us that, despite the inner connection, there exists the distinct possibility of a process of alienation and polarization which could end in total estrangement. During the first twenty years of the existence of Israel as a state, it appears that this has been the dominant process in the life of Israeli Jewish society. The history of Orthodoxy, which has been influenced by the religious definition in its most extreme form, teaches us about the orientation of reserve toward the totality of cultural creativity and toward the full compass of Jewish social life, in favor of those areas which have long been completely encompassed by halakhah and in favor of those sources which do not entail a critical confrontation with the fundamentals of the religion. From this starting point, Orthodoxy naturally arrives at a sharp separateness from the non-Orthodox and nonreligious elements in Jewish society. Eventually there is a threat of a breakdown of the national framework in exchange for a schismatic structure. It seems to be true that this process would lead to a distortion of the original character of the religion, for which Orthodoxy waves the flag. But the possibility that the rift will become a fact is a real danger.

The same is true of the extreme tendencies in the direction of the nationalist definition. Severe, dogmatic objections to religious content also negate the cultural heritage that was shaped by association with that content. Such objections increase the extremist reaction of Orthodoxy. Nationalism itself is then driven to demand separation; a threat develops that the national structure will be broken and replaced by a political, "Israeli" framework. It would seem to be true that this process, too, leads to the uprooting of that ideal for which the proponents of the nationalist viewpoint carry the banner.

The possibility that a rift may eventuate is a real danger. Indeed, even the cultural definition, though it aspired for harmony and compromise, is not free of the rush toward the extremes. It is not by chance, as has been remarked, that the cultural formulation of Jewishness was generally proposed on the basis of the nationalist definition. Preservation of the empty structure created a thrust for providing Jewish content with which to fill it. But this means that the nationalist tendency is based on a drifting away from the religious formulation, while the drifting away finds expression, paradoxically, in efforts to approach and readjust religious values. Thus the attempt to offer the cultural formulation as more inclusive than the religious definition means, in practice, obliteration of the religious character of Jewish tradition and its reassessment as a cultural treasure. But what remains of the tradition when its original character has been obliterated? Fragments of custom and folklore! So even the cultural approach is closed off for the religion, because it leads to alienation from the concept of Judaism as a faith.

From another standpoint, we may ask what remains of a culture whose whole special nature has been given the lie, once religion has been removed from it. A language, a little literature, some customs—and even they become more and more closed off and wrapped in estrangement. Could such a culture, shut off from its origins despite its use of them, have the power to halt the process of polarization and crumbling? The culture itself only exists by virtue of the conflict going on within its own bosom.

IV

Despite it all, the national unity of the Jewish people has been preserved, as has the Jewish identity of its various segments, on the basis of adherence to all those formulations. During the recent past, and for a part of the Jewish community in Israel and the Diaspora this is so even today, these have been authentic expressions of Jewish consciousness. They gave expression to actual conditions, and that was the partial justification of each of them in its place. The Orthodox point of view crystallized out of Jewish piety as a natural and understandable reaction to assimilation, Reform and Conservative Judaism, and secular nationalism. The desertion of Jewish law drove those loyal to halakhah to cling to it just as it was formed in the tradition that came down to them. For them it was like a universal value beyond which there was nothing else. They were moved to protect it against any social process or thought which might bring about change in halakhah, lest its authority be totally undermined thereby. Be that as it may, the embracing of the Jewish way of life that is shaped by halakhah—by that corpus of Jewish law which is the fruit of life within the continuity of a tradition which even great external shocks have not been able to sway—was authentic. This is the secret of Orthodoxy's strength even today.

The extreme nationalist viewpoint crystallized out of the experiment in Jewish assimilation which encountered the opposition of European society. This group held on to its attachment to Judaism while revealing its tragic foreignness in an environment into which it wanted to assimilate. No wonder, then, that it made this experience into the definitive foundation of its Jewish identity. The members of this group clung to the social structure of a Jewry whose fate they shared, though they had no prior basis in either the religious or historical-cultural values of the Jewish masses. It was obvious that the drive for identification could lead to study and immersion in Jewish content. But only in exceptional instances could it bring about a renewed connection with the Jewish religion. At any rate, the consciousness of taking part in Jewish destiny —a consciousness which was the result of direct, terrifying experience—was authentic. And this is the secret of the activist, fighting strength of secular Jewish nationalism to this very day.

Finally, the cultural viewpoint in all its colorations was a typical reaction for those who had been educated in a traditional Jewish home after their faith had broken down. This might have happened through their suffering the burdens of the Jew and the contraction of the Jewish experience in the Diaspora. Or they might have been attracted by European enlightenment without being able to see any opportunity for a place for themselves within European society. This group felt the fate common to the Jewish people as a very powerful traumatic experience. It became so powerful at times that this group verged on revolt against the religious-cultural experience, which, for the group's members, embodied that fate with all the perverseness and deprivation it entailed. But the culturist group also bore within itself a profound store of Jewish education to which it could not be false. It did not formulate its philosophy or way of life by the concepts of that tradition. But it employed fundamentals which it had taken from its Jewish heritage, and it looked upon them as an inseparable part of its intellectual universe. The attempt by such a group to take hold of religious values as a cultural heritage which might define its Jewish identification also seemed natural and understandable in this way. It was the outgrowth of an authentic reality.

Even though an examination of all these definitions of Jewishness raises inner contradictions which cannot be resolved, they were nevertheless valid solutions in their own times because they gave expression to a problematic condition and, at least in part, responded to its difficulties. The trouble is that the personal and historic thrust which gave rise to all these solutions was a centrifugal rather than a centripetal force. They were formulated at the beginning of a process of fragmentation and contraction, not one of unification, attraction, and expansion. They all drew upon certain strata of Jewish life. They all expressed their dynamic in modern times. But they discharged this vast intellectual energy without being able to recharge it through their activity. Without a qualitative tie with the content of the total Jewish heritage, it was not possible to bequeath to the next generation what had been inherited by the first generation—not in extent, not in depth, and not in holding power.

The second generation could not be like the first. They had never known a full Jewish community life conducted according to Jewish law. They had never personally confronted the opposition of European society. They had never sensed their affiliation with the Jewish people with the force of direct personal experience. They had not received a traditional Jewish education in terms of actual obligating values. Judaism was only of historic interest and did not directly touch their lives. Such a generation could never accept any of those formulations as a satisfactory solution that would offer them a valid and all-inclusive tie to Jewishness.

On this basis, such a generation could not identify with the totality of the Jewish people. For by the religious definition, they take part—by direct experience —only in a schismatic structure. Whoever remains outside of that appears to them as an enemy and opponent in the clearest way. By the nationalist definition, they hold membership—by direct experience—in a purely political entity. Whoever remains outside of that appears to them as a stranger with whom one has nothing to do. And the common cultural heritage? Neither the one extreme nor the other will absorb anything of that, except what is grist for their mills, taking the material of tradition into containers that are alien to them and utterly closed off from one another. It is obvious that people who take such an attitude to their tradition will never be able to achieve creative expression through it. They will feel a sense of depressing emptiness, incompletion, and fear of isolation. But perhaps this depression contains something to stir a thought of the need to halt the process of breakdown and alienation. Perhaps it can arouse us to the possibility of speeding up that process of cohesion and rapprochement which is also embodied in the dynamic of Jewish public life. That is a process which could fill all those formulations with significance, even while it brings them back together again.

V

The solution of the problem of Jewish identity on all levels will not be found beyond these three basic formulations. For it is only through them that the Jewish people, in all its various segments, has discovered its unique identification. It is not a new and more inclusive definition which we lack, but a change in our view of the relationship between the existing formulations, as well as a change in the orientation of the activity which is being carried on with these definitions as its basis. We shall never find our way out of the maze until we recognize that all three of these definitions depend for their existence upon the relationship between them. We must come to see that it is their alienation from one another and their mutual opposition that creates conflicts among them and brings about their invalidation.

Such recognition requires fundamental, earnest, purposeful change in the ideological orientation of our social and intellectual activity. Only such a change can lead to a growing openness to replace the obstinacy which has marked the life of the Jewish people of our times. For the devotees of the Orthodox course, this means in practical terms the acceptance, on a clear and positive basis, of the existence of a modern Jewish state and, in the Diaspora, of a Jewish people living within modern society. It further means that they must take their place within the life of the Jewish people in an active manner and make their confrontation with the entire range of its problems.

Such an approach does not necessitate concessions or compromises with their principles. On the contrary, it demands an application of halakhah and religious thought to all areas of the life of modern society. Thus it appears to be more consistent, though harder, than the reserved, separatist approach. Openness and willingness to face things squarely are what created rich strata of culture in the past—along with thought and science, literature, faith, and custom—centered about a life shaped by and based on the tradition of Jewish law. One who takes a position of openness and willingness to confront problems in his environment will again assume possession of that heritage in order to use it as a foundation and to carry on its creativity. Such a culture is a fulfillment without which a complete religious life is an impossibility. But that culture would also offer a broad meeting place for a partnership of creativity and mutual influence between the religious and nonreligious groups. For such a culture can come into being only out of a broad and open confrontation of religion with its world.

For the followers of the nationalist course, this approach demands acceptance of the religious com-

37

munity's existence with an attitude of more than just vague toleration, on the simplistic order of "You live your way and let me live mine." Such a statement is proper for two groups that are living side by side. But it is inadequate for two communities that are trying to live together and become a single entity. If that is the goal, then the secular nationalists must be prepared to take several limitations upon themselves so that people who observe Jewish law may be able to participate actively in every area of life within the society and the State. Thus they may create the condition whereby there can be truly one community. Of course, such a rapprochement will not be possible unless the nationalists alter their approach to religious values and the way of life of the Jewish religion. As long as they regard it as something whose time has passed, whose whole value in the past lay only in the fact that it preserved the Jewish nationality in the Diaspora, no tie on the basis of mutual respect and true understanding between them and the religious community can be possible.

They must learn, therefore, that the Jewish religion is a faith and way of life with independent validity. The nationalists must realize that these religious elements have a significant place within the structure of life in the present. Secular nationalists must confront these values in a relevant manner. Of course, in this confrontation they must stand, first and foremost, for themselves. Contemporary man faces the same questions which religion tried to answer. If he does not accept that answer, he must search for different answers to those questions. This lies at the root of the intellectual dilemma in which the secular community finds itself. And that dilemma will grow as long as they shy away from it.

An attitude of respect and esteem and willingness for relevant confrontation do not mean surrender of values or compromise of principles. They require something much more difficult—consistent fulfillment of what is demanded by humanist philosophy: that the concept of toleration be based on open-mindedness throughout the full compass of a person's intellectual life. Fairness of that magnitude is the precondition for that true culture which the followers of the nationalist course are seeking for the sake of the preservation of Jewish peoplehood, as well as for its own sake. They aspire to the growth of a Jewish humanist culture. But that cannot come into being on the basis of an attempt to swallow up the values of the Jewish religion by falsifying their original meaning. It can evolve only out of direct confrontation with them as values which have present significance.

Even now we are returning to the cultural formulation as a bridge between the extremes. An Orthodox Jew will never reconcile himself to a Jewish nationalism which is empty of any tie to the religion, its viewpoints, and its pathways. A Jewish nationalist may not be able to approach Judaism if that means identifying with its faith and the observance of its ways of life as divine commandments. However, they can open themselves to one another through participation in a culture which reflects the two struggling worlds it contains. And it would even seem that such participation is equally required by a correct understanding of both these approaches.

In this manner, the cultural definition of Judaism is not taken as it is understood in the teaching of Ahad Ha-am and related doctrines. In these doctrines, a historical or biographical relationship to the treasures of the past is required. The adjustment of those treasures to the present is accomplished through a choice made from a point of view that transcends them and by way of an interpretation which cancels out their original meaning, that is, by invalidating them in practice.

Thus the breakdown and alienation we have previously described occurs. The counter-process which aims at recharging the content will bring relevant study and attempts at relevant understanding by both the secular world from the religious viewpoint and by the Orthodox group from the secular standpoint, with the assumption that these worlds touch one another and have significance in one another's eyes. For example, you cannot compare the study of the Bible as a creation, in which the main thing is the religious content and its demand for our understanding and respect, with the study of the Bible as a historic or literary document which contains the "spirit" of our people in the past, or with the study of the Bible by way of shrinking the religious content into social-ethical values. With the first method, the student stands in the presence of the original content and asks what its significance is from his own point of view, even if his approach is critical. With the second, the learner is closed off into his own precincts. He does not reach the heart of the Bible even if his approach is positive—even if it is one of self-identification.

As another example, we may say that you cannot compare a person who asks about the foundations of tradition in order to decorate his life with them, as ornamental elements of folklore, with someone who requires such fundamentals with knowledge of their meaning insofar as they truly express his nature, who refrains from exploiting traditional elements which do not conform with his needs, so as not to degrade them. In the first instance, one grasps the shell and throws away the contents. In the second, one establishes a relationship with what is within, by either the positive or the negative approach. Such an approach neither presumes nor becomes religion. It demands an open mind toward the religious experience and religious thought as things which have meaning, even from the standpoint of someone who is not religious, insofar as he thinks profoundly about himself and his surroundings.

On the basis of such an approach, we should then be able to answer the question: What does it mean to be a Jew? All three definitions are correct insofar as they direct themselves toward one another and strive to meet together in the cultural definition which mediates among them. Being a Jew means belonging to the most inclusive national structure out of loyalty to the Jewish religion, or open-mindedness toward Judaism on the basis of affiliation with the national framework, and participation from both directions in a culture which aims at encompassing all areas of social and intellectual creativity of the entire Jewish community.

Is there any chance of a development in this direction? It was pointed out at the beginning of this discussion that the existence of the Jewish State has worsened and given prominence to the polarization between Israel and the Diaspora, as well as between the sections of the Jewish public in Israel. Let us now point out that the reality of the Jewish State has also awakened a consciousness of the importance of the tie. And it has greatly increased the struggles and the search for ways to return to the tradition as a common foundation. These are two aspects of the same process.

And then there is also this: the reality of a state in which a Jewish community is leading a full and independent life within its own structure is a mandatory condition for the rebirth of a great and complete Jewish culture. In this regard the classic Zionist ideology was, apparently, correct. Its fundamental error was in assuming, in most of its doctrines, that a rebirth would sprout on its own, that for growth one had only to provide the proper external conditions. But such is not the case. Spiritual creativity requires purposeful transmission and conscious nurturing on the basis of a clearly intended decision. This is certainly a process that entails great difficulties. But the potentiality for it exists. The decision is up to us. And the responsibility, for better or worse, will be placed solely upon our shoulders.

3
TRADITIONAL JEWRY
AND THE NONOBSERVANT JEW

I

The tense situation among the sections of Israeli Jewry
has deteriorated to the bursting point in recent years.
One who defines the subject of this tension as merely
a problem between a religious group and a secular
group has made the job easy for himself. He would
naively be accepting an extremistic image which has
been created under extreme conditions. Secular is one
of those words that are used a great deal because they
encompass a periphery of connotations without a fixed
center. You can refer to a subject with them and relate
to it as it appears to you according to your personal
inclinations—all without having to bother to explore
its precise identification. It is possible, of course, that
one should not avoid using such terms in everyday
speech. But in the matter with which we are dealing
here, their undefined use would become an unpardon-
able transgression. The group of persons which is
called secular is not of one mind even with respect to
its attitude toward religion. Furthermore, each individual within the group is not anchored to a fixed set
of attitudes. There is considerable emotional fluctua-
tion from one situation to another, and opinions can
change from one extreme to another. This is especially
true of people who have not crystallized definite

ideologies which would force them to criticize their emotional shifts. Such people are set in energetic motion by transient situations in public or private life.

The same is true of the group called religious. It, too, is not all cut from the same cloth, neither in its views nor in its ways of life. With it, however, we can at least refer to a single stable center. A religious man regards himself as bound by the mitzvot. He attempts to observe Jewish law fully and apply the halakhah to all phases of his activity. (Whether or not he observes this or that commandment is another question. And the way in which he views the matter of halakhah and the manner of its formation is also a question in itself.) This relative definiteness of the term religious certainly enables us to designate what differentiates the groups with a negative definition of secularism from the religious point of view, without falling into the error of employing vague generalities or creating artificial conflicts. The religious person is one who regards himself as obligated to observe the tradition in toto. A secularist is one who does not feel so bound.

This deserves consideration. The negative definition of secularism leaves room for various attitudes toward tradition. These might range from utter indifference all the way to a burning desire to draw near the Jewish heritage and adopt some of its values. For just as the observance of tradition is not always without limits, so nonobservance is not always completely nonparticipatory.

This fluidity in approaches to tradition bears witness that it can be understood properly only in a dialectic manner. Attraction and repulsion are at work within it in various ways, and one cannot grasp attraction without repulsion or vice versa. Typical in this respect is the approach of that segment of the secularist group which, in recent years, has tended to come closer to the tradition. Although it does not represent the entire secularist group—it may actually compose only a small minority—its position nevertheless testifies to a certain general condition.

What has led secularistic Jews, some of whom in their youth even rejected the religious way of life with a forcibly activist negativism, to be attracted again to Jewish tradition? That is a question which has many answers. It is not a subject for discussion in this context. That it is true, at any rate, is clear; and it does not give the impression of being a chance or passing phenomenon. As the years go by, the intensity of the searching for the way back mounts. The tendency toward the production of deeds grows stronger. Of course, these hesitant experimentations do not merit innocent, unequivocal respect. It is not just that the concept of tradition in the minds of these way-seekers is not identical with that of the religious Jew; even their desire to reapproach that tradition is not free of duplicity.

Alienation is a fact which is not easily reversed. And, paradoxically, the desire to overcome it speeds it up painfully. One who seeks to return grasps, with his first step, how far he has unconsciously wandered. In all his pursuits, he is a stranger to the way of life fashioned by tradition. His private and public activity are far away from the interests which tradition embraces. He can no longer stand at his full height within it, nor can he live it to its own maximum. This, then, is the ambiguity expressed in the attitude of those who are seeking ways back. In a general way they favor an attachment to tradition because they comprehend the results of the lack of it and the importance of its role in shaping the human personality. But this generally positive position has no relationship to the definite details with which tradition is involved. They seek tradition, but not precisely this tradition. And thus the generally positive is negated in its application to particulars. From then on, it turns into a selective stand which differentiates what is suitable from what is not suitable in traditional values—on the basis of a yardstick that is external to tradition—until sometimes the affirmation of tradition is made into an actual obliteration of it.

Indeed, this dialectic of attraction within repulsion and repulsion within attraction is also typical of those sections of the Jewish community which display indifference, or even active opposition, to the tradition. The difference between the sections of the secularist group in this regard may be described as one dividing those who recognize the complicated cultural constellation in which they find themselves—and are ready to draw conclusions from it—from those who permit that constellation to determine their own place within it, without giving any thought to the process in which they are involved. Be that as it may, no segment of the secularist community is free of dependence, whether inner or external, on the halakhic tradition. With or without their consent, it is Jewish law which defines their national affiliation.

Membership in the Jewish people entails an indispensable religious condition—this would seem to be undebatable. A Jew can only be someone who at least is not a member of a non-Jewish religion. A change of religion is also a change of nationality. But this condition, which has been defined in the negative, also produces a range of positive conditions. The national unity of the Jewish people depends for its existence on several external marks of identification which come from the body of tradition. Only the most extraordinarily extreme deniers of tradition will be so bold as to reject them. They would include, for example, circumcision, the marriage laws, the dietary regulations, and the observance of the Sabbaths and festivals. Not everyone keeps all of them, but there is no segment of the Jewish community which does not observe a portion of them. In this sense, at least, there is no Jewish group that does not take part in tradition. Thoroughgoing nonparticipation would signify a cessation of membership in the Jewish people, even if no public announcement to that effect was made. It follows, then, that a selective approach to tradition, for whatever reasons—national, cultural, or religious—marks the secularist group in various degrees. Of course, this generalization does not eliminate the importance of the differences among the segments of that group. Nor does it diminish the tension prevailing between the secularist and the religious groups. On the contrary, the tension is sharper just because of this fact. It is this which has created the common ground on which it is possible to speak and clash. It would appear that we can make a general rule: as the common ground contracts, the tendency to clash over it increases and the willingness to talk declines. Only when the area of mutuality is entirely eliminated do both the dialogue and the clash disappear.

It may be said, then, that the national affiliation of a secular Jew depends upon a center located outside the circle of his immediate activity. At the most, his circle intersects the circumference of the life circle of those who observe the tradition. However, he has only the most indirect relationship with the center of that circle. And although he is unable to ignore his dependency, he is fully aware of his alienation. Such is the case whether he deduces from the situation his need to continue being attracted to tradition, or whether he lets things run on as they have been, or even if he revolts against his condition. From this point of view, the observant group, by its very existence, plays a decisive role in the survival of Jewish nationalism. The secularist group acts as a sort of periphery; it is the religionists at the center who provide the nonobservant with a Jewish identity.

But it is obvious that this is only one side of the story. The other side depicts the secularist group as the center of a circle of Jewish life. And this circle defines, though only from the outside, the life circle of the religious group. During the last two hundred years the secular community has been the actively creative element in the life of the Jewish people. This is a fact which, for better or worse, has determined the character of Jewish life in our day. The life of a Jew, even if he keeps the tradition with great meticulousness, has wandered far from the realm which the tradition was able to encompass during the Middle Ages. For without a vast periphery of neutralist secularism, it is impossible to fulfill the mitzvot properly. Ultimately, even the way of life shaped by the halakhah is dependent on something of a political framework. And since the halakhah itself was not able to fashion that framework, Jewish law becomes dependent on something outside itself. The fact that the majority of the religious community does not reject that political structure, and does not look upon it as contrary to halakhah, does not eliminate the structure's externality.

This only goes to show that just as the most indifferent segments of the secularist group participate in the tradition, so do the most extreme elements in the religious community take part in the neutralist secular reality without reshaping it to conform with Jewish law, that is, without internalizing it. It follows that religionists and secularists serve one another as carriers of centers of relationships which, in each case, are determinative for themselves from within and for others from without. It is only the intersected areas on the edges of these circles which alternately expand and contract. What could be easier than to draw from this fact the conclusion that there is a mechanical balance between the two camps? Then each one could be assigned its own role in the preservation of the mutual national structure: this side could become religious functionaries for weekdays, and the other side could be the profane functionaries for holy days. This kind of balance is the basis of the forced political compromise that now exists between the religious and secular parties in Israel, even if no one is brave enough to give it such a theoretical wording. But how dangerous is this odd division. It distorts the truth on both sides. Is it not this which sets up a barrier between the two camps at a point of touchy ambiguity? Is it not this which devises the differences in political structures and prevents movement back and forth? Is it not this which terminates free dialogue by determining beforehand what shall be said on each side?

49

It would seem that true discussion can begin between religionists and secularists only when the dynamic of their relationship is recognized, only when there is a softening of the static fossilization which causes each side to define itself as the antithesis of the other, and only when that stoniness is replaced by a creative development flowing from within and turning outward. A balance of functions is not what is wanted, but rather the realization that there is a common area in which life together is possible. The secular Jew must recognize, and the religious Jew must acknowledge, that tradition is not of less interest to the nonobservant than it is to the Orthodox. And the religious Jew must recognize that secular reality touches him, and that he takes part in its values, no less than does the secularist. Neither political compromise nor mass forgiveness is what is needed—and certainly not a definition of roles which will set up more barriers. Rather, we require more truthfulness in the self-awareness of both religionists and secularists. And we need openness in their relations with one another.

II

The intention of these remarks is certainly not to draw a comparison between the relationships of religionists and secularists to the tradition. Dialectic ambiguity, from which no one is free, includes situations which conflict sharply with one another. In the matter with which we are dealing, the differences are plain to see. Only a community which lives according to the tradition, in the full sense of the word, would be able to create within tradition's realm. A community not living that way might foster a creativity that would be dependent on the tradition or directed toward it. But that creativity would not flow from Jewish tradition or carry it on—quite the opposite. Any attempt on the part of a secular Jew to set forth content in the tradition proper would be an utter blunder. The intent of the preceding analysis was to point out the interconnection of separate situations and to remark on the fact of their being mutually definitive and therefore interdependent. In saying that the secularist group has an independent interest in the tradition and that this interest gives it some rights in this area, our intent was to refer to its interest in what defines its own experience. The secularist has the right to demand that tradition be related to him as he is, with due respect to his values.

And in saying that the religious community has a self-interest in secular existence and its values, we refer to an interest in a reality which embraces the religionist and determines his way of life. The reality of secularism is a religious problem. In our times this problem poses a challenge which has the power to stir creativity in the realm of tradition. At any rate, it is one problem—even if the ways of putting it are many and varied.

To what does that judgment have reference? First and foremost, to the trend toward raging pride in the extremes of both camps: the secularists because of the superiority of their position in shaping the political life of the Jewish people and in creating a secular culture which includes literature, art, science, and education; the religionists by virtue of their superiority in fashioning a way of life with a clear orientation, which the secular community is now rapidly losing. We shall not say very much about the lack of justification for pride

51

from the first direction. It is true, as we have re-marked, that the last two hundred years of Jewish history have been marked by secular creativity and the paralysis of religious creativity. But this secular creativity drew its Jewish character from the tradi-tion. It voiced the struggles of alienation from tra-dition's content and the pangs of existence beyond tradition's realm. And when it had gotten too far away from that content, secularism began to lose its inde-pendence and its worth with frightening speed. The power of tradition was, then, revealed, through the activity of those who drifted away from it and revolted against it. The superiority of which the secularist group boasts, therefore, continually shrinks the more secularism (in the negative sense defined above) in-creases in prominence.

But the pride of the secularists is not a real stum-bling block—because a purely secularist philosophy simply does not exist. Secularism is just the periphery relative to various centers that are located side by side. Its very existence requires neutrality. That is, it requires toleration in the negative and minimal sense of the word: that every person should behave in his own fashion, as long as he does not hurt someone else. Moreover, the more the neutral area of secularism broadens, and the further secularism wanders from the religious and nonreligious centers which originally set it in motion, the more it tends toward complete indifference. Of course, a toleration which comes to mean neutrality or indifference is utterly undesirable. But at least it does not constitute a pitfall.

The main question concerns the religious group, which is not neutral and is certainly not indifferent. Is there any justification for its arrogance? Here, too, the foregoing analysis requires a negative answer. Even if the statement that secularism is involved in a constant process of being emptied of values is correct, the religious group is a party to this process. Orthodoxy has been influenced by it, if only by the religionist's overall dependency on the secular community. Neutralist secularism embraces the religious world; it shrinks and diminishes it. This superiority of which the religious group brags, therefore, dwindles in proportion to the degree in which Orthodoxy closes itself in within its own kingdom—which it does out of fear of the secular reality. It reduces its size the louder it crows about its superiority.

Reflection on the history of Orthodox Judaism bears out the truth of this judgment. Its fanaticism in observing tradition is nothing more than a function of the reduction of its sphere of influence. And even if its loyal children limit their lives in accordance with Orthodoxy's degree of retrenchment, they will not change a thing. Quite the opposite. They are damaging the traditional concept, the essence of which is to encompass the life of a man in all its phases. Orthodox Jews may have iron wills and an admirable degree of resolution. But resolution has its basis in human obstinacy. And that may come at the expense of the acknowledgment of divine authority, before which one is supposed to stand on the basis of freedom.

Of course, there are those who hold to the view that the haughtiness of the religionists is only an expression of a sense of completion and uprightness of stature, that it is only the inferiority of those who are observing them from outside which makes the Orthodox look haughty. But this very assertion is an incarnation of naked arrogance. It expresses the Orthodox person's desire to appear as he would like to be but cannot. This leads to the effort to mold a façade which does not reveal what is inside. Fulfillment and uprightness do not appear in the least as haughtiness, even to an observer who is afflicted with inferiority feelings. Haughtiness is self-assertion against the other person. It imparts a sense of superiority by intentionally downgrading the surroundings and emphasizing the fact that they are being kept at arm's length. More than it bears witness to perfection, then, arrogance testifies to the desire to cover up a weak spot. Indeed, the religious community does possess one superiority which large sections of the secularist group are ready to acknowledge—a clear orientation and a crystallized way of life. But when the religionists boast, they give the lie to their true superiority and reveal their inner weakness. When they operate out of a drive to create, they are no longer able to boast of their superiority to the secular society. For their creations are directed at, and draw their nurture from, secular culture.

III

Restraint of pride would express a thaw in the tense situation. It would lead both sides to acknowledge the existence of common problems which can be solved only by a frank and free interchange. But the question still remains as to whether a free dialogue can take place without both sides being forced to falsify their values or compromise them. This is a question whose solution apparently calls for confrontation between the values, in order to see if they are mutually exclusive. But here, too, we are faced with the fact that there is no one secularist philosophy—just a number of viewpoints. A thoroughgoing confrontation is, therefore, quite impossible. Within the secularist group there are sections which support values opposed to those of the Jewish religion—some which even reject Judaism. However, if we set the religious values side by side with the principles that lie at the foundation of secular society in general—and if those principles are democratic rule and national culture—then from the viewpoint of the secularists no conflict in principle exists.

The question is redirected at the religionist. Can he really take his place without reservation in a framework which embraces both himself and the secular community? Can he take an attitude of true tolerance toward the way of life of a secular person—without derision, without alienation, and a without interfering by coercive methods, directly or indirectly? We must realize that this question does not directly touch on the everyday behavior of the Orthodox Jew. His conduct may be courteous or even friendly, out of personal or social motives. The question affects the overall system of secular reality from the standpoint of halakhic tradition. For that reason, let us reword it. Is a person who does not observe the mitzvot to be permanently and unequivocally labeled as a sinner, according to Jewish law?

At the start it would seem that this question is to be resolved exclusively by halakhic decision; for it is the halakhah which determines the view of the Jewish religion. But this is a mistaken judgment. A halakhic decision is mandatory for those who observe Jewish law. The question which we have raised, however, takes precedence over any halakhic decision. This question relates to what sets the conditions for such a decision. Of course, it is Jewish law which determines the limits of the permitted and the forbidden in the relations between an observant man and a man or community which does not obey the halakhah. However, the label sinner determines not only the relationship of the halakhah to the person so described, but also the relationship of that person to the halakhah. This is an inner determination which deals with the given nature of a reality on which the halakhah must pass judgment. But the relationship of Jewish law to any matter depends not only on the principles of halakhah but also on the character of the given situation. The question, then, is whether the word sinner applies to a secular Jew of our day. Does it describe him correctly in regard to his inner attitude toward the halakhah? This is a question to which any person is entitled to respond, even if he is not an expert in Jewish law. Let the masters of Jewish law step forward and draw their conclusions.

We shall begin by establishing a fact. A Jew who does not observe the commandments in our times does not think of himself as a sinner; and observant people in general do not spontaneously relate to him as if he were. This statement applies not only to the daily contact among people, but also to the broad social interchange between the religious and secular communities. Careful thought might put any religious person into a quandary. But before such thought he does not consider the secular Jew a transgressor. And only rarely does the need arise to examine the propriety of this spontaneous relationship. How is this fact to be illustrated? First of all, by the order of life as it is led in a democratic society.

In a social sense, a transgressor is someone who has

forsaken the observant mass and thereby sinned against the accepted standards of his society. However, such a mass exists only where tradition offers an inclusive structure which determines the life of the society in its totality. That is, the conditions must include a situation where the institutions which represent society fill not only a religious but also a political function. It applies insofar as they fulfill the latter function. The Jewish community up to modern times would be an example of this. In our day the institutions which represent tradition discharge only a partial function. Therefore, one who transgresses against those mitzvot which do not have overall political validity is not regarded as a sinner by the masses. He certainly does not regard himself as a transgressor in his relationship to the community at large. But you will surely be correct if you assert that this category is secondary.

Sin, in its main and primary meaning, is a matter between man and God, not between man and the institutions of society—even if they are institutions which represent religious authority. If it is this category which bears weight, however, a man is still not a sinner unless he has been in a relationship of obligation and violated it. In this sense, sin is the refusal to carry out a commandment—it is not a denial of the obligatory status. If it were possible to posit the existence of a man who was entirely free of obligation, the concepts of holiness and sin would be meaningless for that man. This, of course, is a purely theoretical hypothesis. A man completely free of obligatory status would no longer be a man. Ipso facto, to the extent to which a person does not recognize his state of obligation, these concepts do not apply to him. For this reason, one cannot call a person who is trying to approach the tradition again a penitent sinner. For just as sinner must come before penitent, a sense of obligation is a prerequisite for sin. A penitent does not *approach* tradition. Even when he sins, he confirms the tradition. After all, he is called a sinner only from the standpoint of tradition. But one who feels a need to draw near to the tradition already bears witness against himself that he never violated those commandments from which he was previously alienated. Of course, it is correct to state that the drifting away from tradition on the part of large sections of the Jewish people was, in its day, the result of revolt and rebellion—so at that time it definitely *was* accompanied by a sense of sin. But today the gap is an established fact for which the secular Jew is not responsible. It may be described as a tragedy. It cannot be called a sin. And if something is not a sin, in and of itself, no halakhic decision can turn it into a sin.

It follows that we cannot designate as a sinner someone who does not observe the tradition, except insofar as tradition pertains to him and leads him to it in a bond of obligation. To the extent that tradition performs a general political function, he is subject to it. And to the extent to which he takes part in it on the basis of national awareness or a sense of cultural attachment, he has obligations toward it. In these two senses he may be considered a sinner by himself and the society of which he is a part, when he violates certain regulations. But this is merely a partial tie of obligation. It depends entirely on the historical-cultural situation in which we find ourselves.

Of course, a partial—even a minute—state of obligation opens the way for the establishment of something more inclusive. It is that very possibility which distinguishes the potential relationship of the halakhah to a Jew who is in an obligatory status from the start, and over whom Jewish law has a legitimate demand for obedience, from that of a non-Jew against whom the halakhah has no call—just as he has no tie to it. We do not deny, therefore, the validity of halakhah's claim that every Jew must fulfill the commandments. The secularist Jew must never ignore the legitimacy of that demand in the cultural-national situation in which he himself is placed. However, a justifiable demand and expectation do not necessarily imply hanging the label sinner on somebody. Nor do they mean permission to interfere in the personal and public life of a secular Jew. They simply imply spiritual activity that may go forth toward the secular Jew. The aim of such effort would be to clear from his way obstacles which do not of necessity stem from the nature of tradition. Thus, one may awaken in him a consciousness of obligation which will encompass a larger area than it did before.

This is a tense situation. Possibly it requires a bold step on the part of the halakhists when they define the relation of Jewish law to the incomplete Jewishness of secularistic Jews. At any rate, this situation demands a reexamination of halakhic decisions that were made under different conditions. Such a reexamination is never easy. But boldness now can be the greatest mitzvah. For a continuation of a position which is not directed to the secular Jew, and does not take his true relationship to Jewish law into consideration, will only increase the misunderstanding and widen the tragic gap which, in any case, is already huge.

IV

Good, someone will say; you cannot label a secular Jew as a sinner. However, from the point of view of the Orthodox Jew, the secularist must know that he is in an obligatory status. Does not that point of view require at least an attempt to place the yoke of the commandments on him, directly or indirectly? Does not the religious point of view require that the secular Jew be forced, by various means, to recognize that yoke? This, it would seem, is the problem which troubles both religionists and secularists in the complicated business of their relationship to one another. Whether this is called religious coercion or whether it is emphatically clothed in the more modest terms of legitimate parliamentary politics makes little difference. For the question of the imposition of the mitzvot on nonobservers is a prime controversial issue. It cannot be answered with compromises. Nor can it be squirmed out of by the roundabout methods of pragmatic politics. It must apparently be resolved by the full confrontation of the opposing concepts: individual freedom on one side and divine commandment on the other. Are they really mutually exclusive?

Let us begin by saying something which should properly be accepted as obvious—but in the atmosphere of our mounting misunderstandings, the obvious things have been made obscure. Tradition, of course, includes the commandments to which a Jew is obligated in all areas of his life. But even those who are nonobservant are not devoid of commandments. Though the principle of individual freedom may be the light of their pathways, they feel no contradiction between that and their sense of being under obligation to many mitzvot. What makes trouble for the observant and nonobservant alike is that there seem to be two kinds of mitzvot and that there can be no relationship between a mitzvah within the area of the tradition and another kind of mitzvah.

However, such is not the case. The essence of a mitzvah is the same in any area, even if there are different authorities on which mitzvot are being based. A nonobservant Jew is entitled to voice an opinion in this case, as if he were speaking from the inside, to this effect: being in an obligatory state implies a basic freedom to respond, for if there is no assumption of freedom, there can be no mitzvah. We quote the words of one of the most outstanding sages, Hasdai Crescas, who says in the introduction to his *Or Adonai:* "It will already have been perceived from the meaning of the noun mitzvah, and its definition, that it can apply only to matters where free will and choice operate." Thus we learn that a mitzvah is an act demanded by reason of an authority which we acknowledge willingly. We actualize our freedom by our obedience to the commandment.

When we obey the law out of fear rather than free will—or even if we do so out of routine—we are not at all fulfilling a mitzvah in that way. Of course, there are circumstances in which coercion is justified for acts which, in another context, would be in the category of mitzvot. When the religious command is placed in relationship to areas of social activity where the society has the right of coercion over its citizens, every individual in the society confronts the choice of obeying the laws as mitzvot and thereby actualizing his freedom, or giving in to coercion and thus actualizing his subjection. Therefore, wherever the institutions which represent religious tradition exercise a

61

political function, they may legally employ coercion.
But the authority has been given them as political and
not religious institutions. The justification they have to
use coercion in religious matters, insofar as they have
such justification, is political, not religious. In the area
of actual religious affiliation, there is no room for coercion. Religion knows only mitzvot. Reward and punishment are inherent in the commission or omission,
as derived from the demand to fulfill the commandments for their own sakes.

Coercion, then, not only stands in conflict with the
vague assumption of individual freedom. It conflicts
with the well-defined assumption of a bond of obligation between man and his Creator. An attempt to
compel the fulfillment of a divine commandment is an
immediate contradiction. Furthermore, in an era
when religious institutions do not perform a political
function, coercion on their part has no political justification. Attempts in that direction are therefore in the
category of grave perversion, from any point of view.
Is someone who is forced to rest against his will on the
Sabbath fulfilling a mitzvah—or could that be said of
someone who, by resting, is obeying a law of the State?
Can someone who forces his will upon others on the
basis of arbitrary power be fulfilling a commandment
of God? It would appear that nowhere is the dividing
line between fulfillment and distortion of the mitzvah
narrower than in the actions of observant Jews. They
pass judgment where judgment does not belong to
man. Their intransigent willfulness separates them
from their Creator.

We must admit that from the viewpoint of an observant Jew, every Jew stands in a condition of obligation. Obliged, but not forced. The right and even the

mitzvah of arousing one to his duty flow from this judgment. However, the appeal to one's fellowman to arouse him must be done by way of a full and direct relationship to his humanity, on the basis of respect for his views and with care lest he be deprived of his freedom.

V

Once we have removed the obstacle of coercion, we are faced with the duty of defining the meaning of toleration in the relations between observant and nonobservant Jews. If we were speaking of two clearly distinguishable groups, each living its own special life side by side with the other, the vague formulation held to by many of the nonreligious group would suffice. "You live your way and let me live mine." But observant and nonobservant Jews, whether they like it or not, share many areas of life. That vague definition of tolerance no longer offers a solution. On the contrary, it immediately deteriorates into an open display of a lack of willingness to understand the other side and give it consideration. Toleration requires a meeting among people, not a mutual self-segregation, with each one in his own armor.

If we were speaking of two clearly distinguishable groups whose contact was limited to narrow areas of economic and political activity, it might be different. We might follow those who want to separate religion from the State, limit the frame of obligations which are to apply to the masses, and permit each segment of the public to conduct itself in its own way. But we have already emphasized that the relationship between the observant and the nonobservant is not subject to circumscription or restriction. It takes in all areas of social activity, and it sets up the most inclusive framework of national affiliation. There is mutual dependency between the two sides. Any attempt, therefore, to cut off their contact with one another places the unity of the Jewish people in doubt and endangers its very existence.

In such a situation we must not be satisfied with a negative formulation of toleration, as if it were a negative commandment to refrain from inflicting injury. We must define it positively, as a positive commandment to move toward the other side, so that a shared existence may become possible. For example, it is fitting for those in the nonreligious group, though they have no tie to religion for its own sake, to accept cheerfully the burden of many regulations which create the conditions for national unity and continued existence. These would include the marriage laws, observance of the dietary laws in public institutions, observance of the Sabbath and festivals in public institutions, and the like. Furthermore, such consent from the nonreligious community should properly be given voluntarily, on the basis of its own interests and views. It should not have to come as a result of political pressure. If arrived at in the right way, such agreement would remove the bitter taste of coercion. Then much of the hesitancy would disappear from both sides. It would seem that the nonreligious community has good reason to grant general applicability to several religious regulations and public protection to others— if only out of recognition that this is a condition for the unification of the nation. It should not be necessary to bring this about against the will of that community. We have already pointed out that, even from the viewpoint of a very limited nationalism, tradition is not the sole interest of the religious group. This is all the more true from the standpoint of cultural Jewish identification. The nonreligious groups have an interest in fostering the observance of tradition.

We may go so far as to say that if these laws were accepted, the secular community would acquire the right to make demands on the tradition. Secularists would no longer leave it thoughtlessly to the exclusive interest of those who represent it in political life. Tradition affects the life of secular Jewry. Just as the secularist has an interest of his own in maintaining tradition, he also has an absolute right to make demands on it. The upholding of tradition and its susceptibility to demand are indivisible. Under what conditions? When we speak in terms of the value system of every secular person. If his move in the direction of the tradition and its representatives flows from his own values and interests, it is not to be considered a compromise. By necessity, he takes his stand before tradition with his full stature. He cannot be asked to compromise on anything, great or small, for there can be no compromise on the preservation of values. The observers of tradition are also required, then, to move toward the other side. This move is also necessary for their own interests, if only out of concern for the unity of the State. For the State of Israel, it would seem, is a religious mitzvah no less than it is a national value.

Indeed, the nonobservant Jew's demand that the Orthodox take a direct, respectful attitude toward secular values is the challenge which the secularist hurls at the religionist. With that demand he also performs an important task from the point of view of the tradition itself. Response to this demand leads to a confrontation with the whole range of activity of contemporary man. Such a confrontation is needed by the tradition. To the degree to which tradition is faithful to its ambition to embrace all phases of human activity, and to avoid placing limitations on any positive creative force, it requires this confrontation. If a person cannot stand at his full height within the realm of tradition, that tradition has become fossilized at the hands of its representatives and guardians. It is for this reason that traditional Judaism must turn to the realm of those who are not observant—not just because of the need for the preservation of national unity, but also on account of the inner logic of the religious life.

Perhaps, finally, it is not superfluous to note that willingness of the representatives and devotees of tradition to confront the reality in which, like it or not, both they themselves and nonreligious Jews are living may not only prevent friction and pave the way for cooperative work, but may also open the door for those members of the secularist group who are searching for a path of approach to the tradition. There are a limited number of ways by which the vast gap between nonreligious Jews and the way of life shaped by halakah can be bridged. (1) The halakhah must be made to take a positive view of all the areas of life to which modern Jewish existence has given rise, whether they have come into being because of the conditions of modern life or because of the establishment of the State of Israel. (2) There must be an attempt from the halakhic direction to surmount the restrictions which create a moral dilemma, not only for the nonreligious, but also for the Orthodox person who is not prepared to live in a condition of contra-

diction between his religion and his moral convictions.
(3) There must be a willingness to make room for
every kind of creative human activity within the
realm of halakhah.

It becomes more and more apparent that this gap is
not the result of conflicting viewpoints, nor is it even
a matter of lack of faith. Its source is the vast estrangement in ways of life. If Orthodox Jews themselves give
some thought to their own way of life, they may thus
narrow that gap. They can turn the religious community into a shiningly effective center of attraction for
the secularists. Under what conditions would this apply? If the religious community would relate to secular reality and not build fortresses against it.

Tolerance, when understood in an active sense, is
neither a compromise nor a concession—quite the opposite. It is creative action in which humanity is revealed in all its power and at its full stature. Of course,
it demands no less of the other fellow than that with
which it responds to *his* demands. Is the nonreligious
group prepared to display such tolerance? We may,
apparently, reply to this question in a generally positive way. Large sections of that group are showing
sympathy for tradition. Even if one differs with their
method and view, still the very tendency they are
revealing testifies to a willingness, the meaning of
which has not yet been properly evaluated by the
Orthodox section.

But is the observant community ready for the same
thing? One can only answer this question doubtfully
yet hopefully. To tell the truth, it is upon that community that, from the spiritual viewpoint, the hardest
part of the task must fall. And, sad to say, it is not
displaying many signs which would bear witness to an

ability or willingness to discharge this responsibility. But woe to the Orthodox group if this opportunity does not awaken an ability to translate the potentiality into reality. And woe to us all if, instead of spiritual work, there will come the politicians' routine and the fanatics' irascibility.

4
A SECONDARY RELATIONSHIP TO TRADITION—A STUDY OF ONE PARTICULAR ASPECT OF AHAD HA-AM'S DOCTRINE

I

The secular Jew's attitude toward the tradition is not necessarily a negative one. He frequently desires not to be cut off from it, whether he is looking for support for his opinions and actions in it, or whether he is fulfilling some parts of it. Even when he is showing an interest in traditional values, however, his attitude to them is, for the most part, a secondary one. He attaches importance to the very preservation of the connection between tradition and himself in such a form. But this importance does not originate in an allegiance to tradition's values, but rather in tradition's role in preserving national unity, or even because of tradition's utility in certain social or personal situations. A secondary tie, then, represents an attitude toward tradition as a means; it features a functional attitude, indifferent to the values under consideration when they are viewed as ends in themselves.

It is to be understood that the term indifference does not characterize the emotions of the secular Jew. His feelings may be quite warm and cordial. But in thus relating matters to each other our intention is not to describe emotions, but the manner of their application to their subject. It is quite possible that indifference to tradition's values might lead to an emotional expression, like praise or the attribution of superiority, or to something like longing or the pain of alienation. However, we shall not miss the truth if we state that an emotional relationship is in itself an embodiment of a secondary attitude. It is typical of the person who has drifted away from actions or ideas that once played a decisive role in his life. His relationship to them expresses the fact that they no longer fulfill the same function for him and that it is all purely a matter of the past. It is like an object which a person keeps from his youth because of the memories it holds.

The emotional attitude of the secular Jew toward the tradition is, then, essentially a secondary one. It has its origin in the function which tradition fulfilled, or could have fulfilled, in his life. His longing turns his feelings, not to its specific values, but to the condition of life generally to be connected with tradition. For he feels the lack of it even when he is alienated from it.

Of course, this relationship's illumination of tradition and search for it contains a special importance for the doctrine of Ahad Ha-am. In his statements we find an instructive ideological, if nonmethodical, development of the secondary attitude toward tradition. Furthermore, his influence has had a wide effect. Even today, many of his ideas on this problem have a decisive influence on the thought processes of secularists who are searching for a basis in tradition despite their alienation from it.

A perspective analysis of these views in the doctrine of Ahad Ha-am therefore offers a certain amount of illustration of several typical features of the Jew who, even today, is trying to determine the nature of his connections with Jewish tradition.

II

The secondary attachment to tradition finds expression in the thought of Ahad Ha-am in the major premise of his theory of nationalism. This premise assumes that a nation, like an individual, has a will to survive and that that will can be used as the means of explaining everything that happens in the nation's history. And, indeed, the nation is frequently described in Ahad Ha-am's philosophy as an organic entity. The will to survive which courses through it is what motivates it in every situation it experiences. The culture which it creates is but the chronicle of encounters in various fateful circumstances, or, more precisely, it reflects the nation's will to live through those circumstances. It follows that the manifestations of the national culture, though they are of varied colorations, are always connected with a single center of gravity. That point is the "national ego" which persists in protracting its existence. Those cultural manifestations, therefore, have a common denominator from the point of view of the function they fulfill. Their value is repeatedly reexamined from a functional standpoint with these questions: Are they still serving the national will to survive? Are they still performing their primary role or has their time passed?

This, it would seem, is why Ahad Ha-am hardly ever approaches a basic, all-inclusive theoretical analysis of any specific cultural feature of Judaism in his writings. Nor does he aspire to characterize Judaism as a complete system or a crystallized philosophy by giving a harmonious interpretation or a proposed synthesis between the various fundamental features and their opposites, both of which Judaism contains. The common factor in all cultural manifestations exists, for him, beyond such a theoretical discussion and outside the circle of values of overall Jewish culture. No matter how widely those cultural features vary, all of them represent the amplitude of the will to survive of the national ego. Such is the root of their unity—beyond any value difference among them. If such be the case, then the relationship of the secular Jew to these cultural manifestations should also be determined on the basis of that same functionalist criterion. He must show his loyalty, not because he derives his philosophy of life from the concepts of tradition or fashions his life according to it, but because of the function those concepts fulfilled in the past life of the nation and because of the national will to survive which continues to throb within him.

This, then, is the major premise: Existence itself takes more than substantial precedence over the content of the culture and the tradition, because it is the source of the content. This is an assumption to be found at the base of the philosophy of nationalist thinkers in contemporary Judaism. They place the will to continue existing as a nation in the category of superior value. And on that basis they set forth the need to cling to tradition, even before giving an opinion about the actual content of the Jewish heritage. The need for a connection with tradition is not expressed by the essence of the content to which one must be connected. It preexists them, and *in this sense* it is indifferent to them.

Later we shall see that from this premise there flow several consequences which are also shared by Ahad Ha-am and, consciously or otherwise, by a great many of his disciples.

III

If we wish to grasp the conclusions of the will-to-survival postulate as a point of origin for a study of the intellectual creativity of the Jewish people, we must give some thought to Ahad Ha-am's well-known essay *Avar Veatid* (Past and Future). It is one of a group of short articles in which Ahad Ha-am appears as a systematic thinker, who proceeds from initial assumptions to the conclusions that are to be derived from them. Of course, one who studies these essays deeply can convince himself that this outward appearance is deceptive. It reflects stylistic, not theoretical, considerations. At any rate, the systematic does not typify Ahad Ha-am's manner of thinking. The external structure hinders more than it helps in properly understanding his emphases. Ahad Ha-am has only an apparent interest in the universals which he posits in the relatively long introductions to his essays. To tell the truth, he is interested in the tangible particular for which the universal has been created. And, indeed, anyone who reads these essays to learn matters of general consideration is destined to be bitterly disappointed. He will quickly discover that their generalizations are vague and unfounded. However, the reader may be greatly rewarded if he gives attention to the practical detail for which the generalization was invented. Ahad Ha-am's practical assertions are always most instructive, even when they are open to attack from various sides.

In this sense, the essay *Avar Veatid* is an illuminating example. It works from the definition of the individual ego as a combination of past and present, that is, of memory and hope. The ego persists as long as the rememberer is a hoper. Forgetting cuts off the continuity of self-awareness, and in this sense it is the end of the ego; the loss of hope bears witness to a diminution of the instinct for survival—and that means death. The same holds true for the nation. The only difference which Ahad Ha-am designates between nation and individual is that a physiological organism has infancy, childhood, and old age, with its course completed in one cycle. A social organism, however, while it may go through the same kind of cycle, is able to renew its youth several times. The future of the individual is limited, while the future of the nation is limitless.

The easiest thing is to prove that the more these assumptions of Ahad Ha-am are taken as universals, the more they become vague and groundless. But anyone who gives thought to their manner of formulation will be convinced that the thinker's interest was not at all directed toward them. He flits about on all sides of his subject so as to choose just that one aspect which will be right for his practical interest. Indeed, once the reader focuses his attention on that practical interest, he understands even this one-sided selection and arrives at a full comprehension of the author's intention.

Ahad Ha-am's interest in this essay is to combat two diametrically opposite tendencies in the Jewish community of his time: a casual abdication of any tie to the treasures of the Jewish past, on one hand, and, on the other, a stagnant attachment to the dregs of the past. One side forgot history and ignored the Jewish heritage; the other side rigidly refused to understand the circumstances of the modern age and to adjust to them. It was Ahad Ha-am's feeling that the people of Israel had been placed in jeopardy of losing its identification by both these extremes. Forgetting the past meant cessation in the continuity of the national consciousness, and final assimilation; while a stagnant orthodoxy, freezing the lees of yesteryear, would also cut off communication between the younger and older generations. The former would assimilate, the latter would wither away.

Ahad Ha-am was therefore searching for a middle way between memory and hope. More precisely, he wanted a path between loyalty to the heritage of the Jewish past and willingness to adjust to the conditions of modern life which require the Jew to put the traditions of his past to a new test. The results of this test could be quite revolutionary. The desire to impart a theoretical justification to this middle position was what drove Ahad Ha-am to erect high-flung, teetering domes of generalization on his down-to-earth foundation. By placing the generalization next to the practical underpinning, however, we come out all the richer. For the universal defines, with exceptional clarity, the change in the relationship of the Jew to his tradition. What was once a relationship of obligation in practice now becomes one of remembering. For Ahad Ha-am, the relationship to tradition took the form of a relationship to the past as a value system from which the contemporary Jew had already grown distant. But in his intent expectation for the future, he was refusing to part with his heritage so as not to lose his self-identification. In this sense Ahad Ha-am's generalization is neither vague nor baseless. It faithfully expresses a quite definite spiritual condition.

Ahad Ha-am speaks for his generation. It was a generation educated in the traditional Jewish schooling. Its members were taught by the tradition and cut off from it in their youth. From then on, tradition formed a stratum, perhaps the decisive stratum, in their makeup. But it was never spread before them as a set of values with practical significance, nor did it ever shape their way of life. It could comprise an important part of one's personal biography. It could, for example, be a complex of facts in one's memory. And that complex could contain material to shape a person's character indirectly. It could furnish him with a store of association from which he could nurture himself. But it would never be part of the views which guided him directly in his everyday conduct of life. Such a relationship to tradition did not permit disavowal. One cannot disavow his past without paying for it with an unauthentic life that is overlaid with pretense. One does so at the price of having to force oneself both within and without. (Ahad Ha-am well described the lack of authenticity in the life of Western Jewry in his famous essay *Avdut Betokh Kherut* [Slavery in the Midst of Freedom].) But at the same time one cannot turn this past into an integral part of his daily existence. It remains a shadow that dogs his footsteps wherever he goes, a shadow from which he cannot gain freedom without losing the body that casts the shadow. But after all is said and done, it is still nothing but a shadow.

It must be said that the relationship to tradition is made secondary when it is taken as a tie to a heritage from the past. What I was does not determine what I am now, except in a roundabout causal way. It may explain me and give me significance, but it does not define my present condition. This is a relationship which carries on the continuity of self-awareness as a range of situations which the consciousness has experienced. But it persists solely in the memory. In regard to the perpetuation of continuity, the very fact of remembering has decisive importance. But the content in which the memory is embodied is incidental to it. The content is necessary for the survival of the memory as a vital function in the life of the personality, but it is not required in and of itself.

The essay *Avar Veatid* was therefore intended to propose an all-inclusive theoretical justification for a secondary relationship to the tradition. Indeed, its vast influence on broad circles of secular Jewry to this very day is inherent in this fact. Loyalty to the past is interpreted by them as a conclusion drawn from their desire to lead an authentic existence. They are saying: "We cannot *deny* what we were, even if we are *revolting* against what we were." Our history is a part of our being. It explains us. It carries within itself the conflicting currents of the continuity of our own consciousness. Such is our motive for learning and remembering it. The duty to know the past is decreed by the great imperative "Know thyself." For self-knowledge lays down the conditions for survival of the self. This seems to be a normal assertion in discussions on questions of the acquisition of Jewish knowledge and Jewish education in general.

IV

A relationship to the spiritual creativity of the Jewish people as part of the content of the memory accounts for the resulting sharp change in evaluation of the meaning of tradition in general. Here we encounter a typical vagueness in the meaning of concepts. This confusion has a recognizable history in several of the outstanding movements in modern Jewish thought.

77

The idea of "tradition" is swallowed up in that of "culture" until it is almost undifferentiated as a separate subject.

A marked example of such blurring is found in Ahad Ha-am's essay *Mukdam Umeukhar* (Early and Late). There he distinguishes early ideas, which appeared before the conditions for observing and understanding them had ripened, from late ideas, where the conditions that had required their observance had disappeared. The late ideas, however, nevertheless deserved preservation for the sole reason that the time might again come when use would be found for them. What was early for its time should be kept until its day dawned, and what was late should be retained until suitable conditions once more arose. It is easy to see that at the foundation of this assertion lies the doctrine of the national will for survival, which makes use of various kinds of instruments—all in accordance with the circumstances of time and place.

But though the will to survive is set forth as sole justification for the preservation of laws and concepts, there is also indirectly specified here a certain understanding of the tradition. It is presented as an accumulation of the riches of the spirit, layer upon layer. These are riches which memory preserves, raising them into active existence in the hour of need and then pushing them back into the passive memory afterwards. In other words, tradition does not have the status of an actual obligation which is applicable at all times. It is, rather, a pool flowing from the creativity of earlier generations to the members of every successive generation. They select from the pool only what is right for themselves. Later we shall see that in regard to the act of choice it is less a matter of conscious deliberation than one of direct absorption. It is the kind of thing for which a person does not always give an account to himself. After the fact, he has taken what his own character and that of his environment influence him to take. Ahad Ha-am, then, makes no differentiation between the overall spontaneous attachment of a man to his culture and his relationship to tradition. The concept of an obligation in respect to an actual authority is erased without any discussion. In this manner, the tradition empties all its content into the storehouse of the culture and is lost to view.

Indeed, this is the postulate on the basis of which we may most clearly comprehend Ahad Ha-am's statements when he comes to formulate his relationship to the tradition in his especially important essay *Divre Shalom* (Words of Peace).

Ahad Ha-am's first intention in *Divre Shalom* was to escape the accusation of being a Reform Jew or Karaite, which could be leveled at him on the basis of a misunderstanding of his views. He first distinguishes Karaism and Reform. Karaism is not a reform of the religion. It is a complete denial of part of Judaism, together with a rigid observance—with no thought of reform—of the part which is not denied. Reform Judaism means the acceptance of all parts of the religion accompanied by the intention of reforming all of them. This description of Reform Judaism supplies Ahad Ha-am with formal grounds on which to oppose it. Reforming a religion while confessing it is, to him, a contradiction in terms. For you cannot acknowledge an authority while at the same time regarding yourself as having authority over it. Have you not, by your very intention of reforming the religion on your own, denied its authority? This reasoning appeared so decisive to Ahad Ha-am that he never bothers to reexamine whether it is properly directed against the actual views of the reformers. Nor does he require any further grounds in order to demolish the structure of Reform Judaism.

This stand, even though it is baseless, at least bears witness to the powerful faith of its proponent. He understands that religion is based on authority and that the authority cannot be undermined without upsetting the entire religion. The trouble is that he himself no longer admits the authority. He can only speak in the second person. He can only make a conditional acknowledgment which casts a bright light on the delicate circumstance in which Ahad Ha-am finds himself, as a cautious, conservative thinker. Of course, he is sincere when he proclaims that he is not interested in the destruction of the religion and that he is not a supporter of Reform. But his interest in the preservation of Judaism proceeds from a reason that does not coincide with that of observant Jews, though he well understands the logic of their system. He takes his stand on a different basis, from which he defines the difference between himself and rabbinic Judaism. Instead of speaking of a reform of Judaism, therefore, he speaks of its development.

What, then, does development mean, and how is it different from reform? From Ahad Ha-am's statements in this essay, one may learn only that the difference between reform and development is not one of content, but of manner of occurrence. Reform is conscious change, development is unconscious. In reform, there is an undermining of authority. In development, no such undermining occurs, because the adjustment to new circumstances takes place on the basis of the fiction of continuity without change.

These statements place Ahad Ha-am in a strangely forced state of confrontation toward his rabbinic opponents. He cannot deny their position because, by his system, he must affirm the thought process which they follow in their system. If he really wants Judaism to develop through the agency of its legitimate representatives, he must not want them to recognize that the religion is indeed developing; yet he is obligated to explain to them his opinion that there is a development in the religion, even when those who are fostering it are unaware of it.

Does not this forced situation bear witness to the shakiness of Ahad Ha-am's interpretation? Does it not cast doubt upon the very assumption of unconscious change in the area of tradition? These are questions which go far beyond the scope of the present work. However, at least a word of conclusion may be written here. The theory of the unconscious development of Judaism completes the blurring of boundaries between culture and tradition, while at the same time pointing up the difficulties that issue from this confusion. Unconscious absorption and unthinking change are typical of an attachment to a culture from which a person takes according to his inclinations and capabilities, without bothering to give himself an account of how and why he has taken or altered or neglected it.

A tradition which is understood as a content of memory is thus made into one of the strata of a culture from which each Jew may draw sustenance according to his own manner and ability.

81

V

A secondary attachment to tradition leads, then, to an evaluation of tradition as just one equally worthy part of a cultural heritage. In this respect Ahad Ha-am presents a characteristic view of secularist Jews, or of Jews who are standing on the threshold of secularism. For example, take the attempt by Chaim Zhitlowsky, in his later articles, to make an approach to tradition. He saw it, not as the embodiment of religious values, but as the seat of cultural content. His orientation was toward neutralizing the content in respect to its connection with religious values. In contrast, Conservative Judaism in the United States, and in particular the experiment of Mordecai Kaplan, attempted to grasp the religious values themselves as cultural content, apparently without "neutralizing" them. Or contemplate the repeated attempts on the part of secular Jews to adapt traditional values, like the Sabbath and festivals, and to consider them not as religious commandments, but as cultural content which they take pleasure in honoring.

In all these examples there operates, explicitly or implicitly, that postulate for which Ahad Ha-am serves as spokesman in *Divre Shalom*: a person may tie himself to traditional values to the degree that he understands them in a cultural sense. This leaves him freedom of choice toward them. Thus we have a view which permits one to leap "spontaneously" and "unconsciously" (that is, without paying attention or recognizing obligation) over the original meaning of the values of the tradition so as to take a secondary and functional attitude to them.

But here is the consummate question in this problem of the relationship of the secular Jew to the tradition. Is it really possible to adapt its values as the content of a culture without robbing them of meaning even in their new role? Is tradition still tradition, and —even more—does it contribute anything to the storehouse of culture, once one regards it functionally and denies it its authority?

To be completely truthful, we must say that Ahad Ha-am's words describe his own relationship, and that of many of his contemporaries, to the tradition. After the fact, he is still connected to it by a memory which has shaped his intellectual world, even though traditional values are no longer directly included in his views and patterns of living. As far as he himself is concerned, the solution that he proposes is nothing more than the statement of an unchallengeable fact. However, it is a fact only because Ahad Ha-am's attitude toward tradition was formed in his early years, not on the basis of a secondary-functional attachment, but in a direct relationship of acknowledgment of an authority. That is not true of the secular Jew who was not reared in a traditionally observant home. For him, the content of this tradition is not a matter of personal memory. Thus he cannot relate to it even culturally. As far as he is concerned, a secondary relationship is like no relationship at all. This is the reason that forces him to pose again the question with its full bite and to wrestle with it directly, outside the circle of solutions of Ahad Ha-am and of those who routinely walk his path.

5

PARTIAL OBSERVANCE
OF THE TORAH'S COMMANDMENTS

The following statements are made from a personal point of view. It is the point of view of a Jew who was not educated according to the halakhah. Nor, if he is judged by the accepted standard of Israeli society, is he to be classified as a religious person. But certain experiences, and the spiritual development to which they gave rise, have brought him into a fresh confrontation with the tradition. He is searching for a way to return to it, be obligated under it, and live in accordance with it.

I shall not enter into an analysis of the causes of this development. That is quite a broad problem and would, in and of itself, require a separate discussion. I assume, however, that this point of view does not express the position of just some marginal individuals, but is a typical stand which derives from the cultural situation of a generation whose problems we must meet.

Any Jew who wishes to return takes his stand before the tradition in an ambivalent position. He wants to establish contact with it; but just when he tries to carry out his wish, he discovers how far he is from the tradition and how far it is from him. It contains so much that is strange. There is strangeness of life and thought patterns. For that reason, he is unable to accept it in totality. And if it is demanded that he accept and fulfill everything as a condition for rapprochement, he pulls back again. The only possibility open to him is that of selecting part of the whole. So he asks whether this is a legitimate stand. Is he really approaching tradition by making his selection? Or is he, perhaps, only deceiving himself in vain, because his partial acts have no religious significance? If the answer to his original question is affirmative, what method of choice would not violate a correct conceptualization of the Jewish religious tradition? I shall try to answer these questions.

I begin with a definition of the subject of mitzvah as I understand it. A mitzvah is a directive given us by someone other than ourselves, ordering us to behave in a certain manner out of a recognition of the authority of the one who gives the mitzvah. By this definition, a mitzvah is not accompanied by any element of compulsion. A person who recognizes the authority of the orderer is obligated, but not forced, to carry out the order. He is under a demand to act out of a decision of his own free will and accord. Reward or punishment is contained in the action or the failure to act. This is all in the category of the principle "The reward of a mitzvah is—a mitzvah." If we are speaking of a religious mitzvah, through which a person finds himself in the presence of his God, we then mean a directive whose source is in a divine authority whose presence we are in at the moment we give our obedience as an act of free will.

This definition brings us, at the start of any discussion of the observance of the commandments of Judaism, face to face with the problem of acknowledging the principle of the divine origin of the Torah. I have no

intention here of injecting myself into a detailed discussion of this principle. Our canvas is quite limited.
However, I have to state that belief in this article of
faith and in the conclusion that derives from it—that
all the commandments of the Torah, both written and
oral, are binding because they are God's commandments—is for me a precondition for a true approach
to tradition. This is so because the denial of this principle obliterates the very concept of tradition. So even
if a nonbelieving person fulfills a part of tradition's
directives, he is no longer fulfilling them as mitzvot.

On the other hand, I must stress that the sense of the
concept of divine origin of the Torah, and the essential
meaning of the revelation at Mount Sinai as a historical event, are not among the things most completely
agreed upon in the chronicles of Jewish thought.
Many approaches exist on this matter, and each person may find his own special path for it. It is clear that
one's consciousness of obligation toward the totality of
the commandments of the Torah is dependent—in
both the interpretation of the meaning and in the
understanding of the conditions, manner, and details
of their application—on the way in which he takes this
principle.

I opened this chapter by laying down the conditions
for a proper return to the tradition with the most
all-embracing profession of the divine authority of the
Torah. Now I must comment on what might be
viewed as a contradiction of this postulate; but it really
appears to me as an inevitable conclusion from it.
While the general fulfillment of the Torah's commandments requires this overall admission, it necessitates also an interpretation of more than the reason for
the mitzvah and of the conditions and manner of its

application. Without these things the mitzvah is entirely unobservable. But an ongoing process of selection from the totality is also called for. And this selection is to be made in accordance with the changing conditions and objectives of the Jewish community and the individuals living within it.

From this point of view, it seems to me that the difference between those Jews who call themselves Orthodox and the Jew who keeps only a part of the commandments, according to the choice which I intend to propose later, is not a difference of principle but one of condition. Of course, the importance of this difference is not to be denigrated nor its meaning ignored. But it does not erect an impassable barrier between them.

It would seem that only a very few people would argue against the assertion that the observance of a mitzvah necessitates its interpretation. This is, after all, the basic assumption for the diversion of written Torah from the oral Torah. It is the basis for the continual growth of the oral Torah. And it is that which gives the Torah to every generation in keeping with its situation and the conditions of its existence. For this reason I shall not belabor this point. I shall pass on to the second part of the foregoing assertion, which will surely stir controversy. It states that the fulfillment of a mitzvah is possible only in accordance with a definite choice of a part from the whole.

This choice is, in my opinion, made from two points of view, but the two are closely connected: (1) the external choice, made in keeping with personal, social, political, and perhaps also "objective" cultural circumstances; and (2) the inner choice, made in keeping with the inner disposition of the life of the personality in the broadest possible sense. It is clear that there is a connection between the external circumstances, especially the social and cultural ones, and the inner disposition of the personality. For we are not discussing tendencies of a capricious nature. Indeed, it also seems to me that in the external timing of the mitzvot, things are more or less agreed upon. Every commandment is applicable to us in its own special time, place, circumstances, and manners. Its observance depends upon the correct conjunction of those conditions. More precisely, it depends on our being convinced that these conditions exist.

It is taken for granted that a Jew is obliged to anticipate the timing of mitzvot and, if he can, to bring them on by his own actions. But this is not always within his power. Much depends on outer circumstances over which he has no control. In such an event, it may be said that one's very willingness to fulfill the commandment is credited to one as if it had actually been carried out. From another point of view, it is clear that the decision as to whether the conditions under which these commandments devolve upon us are present or not depends, in many instances, on the interpretation we give them. Thus the boundary between "outer readiness" of the mitzvah to be performed and "inner readiness" to perform it is not at all clearly marked.

We now come to the hardest question of all: the nature of and criteria for the choice in accord with one's inner readiness. It is legitimate for me to ask whether a certain mitzvah applies to me under a given set of external circumstances. It is equally in order to put the question as to whether, given my spiritual and intellectual state, the mitzvah applies to me in the fashion in which it is formulated in the written or oral Torah, as it has come down to us from earlier generations. There can be changes in the external set of life situations which cause the fulfillment of certain commandments to become impossible. Or the fulfillment of those mitzvot might bring about a result different from what was originally intended. That is obvious. But it must likewise be said that there can be changes in one's inner set, because of which a person might be unable—subjectively speaking—to fulfill certain commandments; or fulfilling them might stir emotions or thoughts within one that could be different from, or even the opposite of, that which was originally intended.

It has already been remarked that external change has significance in regard to the applicability of the mitzvah. This is true not only because of the physical conditions which foster or hinder its observance, but also by reason of the implications the mitzvot have for the life of the society and the state, and even for the spiritual and intellectual life of the individual. If it is legitimate to examine the validity of the mitzvah in accordance with its meaning for the life of the society, it must also be legitimate to test its applicability in terms of the inner disposition of the life of the spirit.

This kind of test is especially pertinent if we are speaking of commandments which shape or express one's inner relationship to God. Then we may ask whether or not the person is able to regard himself as prepared for that mitzvah. For if he is not so prepared, even if he stubbornly performs an act, it is doubtful that he can thus be considered as having carried out a commandment. It is possible, then, that one of two things may happen. Either the person may not have attained the mitzvah because the proper conditions have not matured within him; or the mitzvah has not come through to him, that is, it has not been interpreted or applied to the reality in which he is situated.

Since these statements are far from being generally agreed upon, I would like to prevent the misunderstanding that crouches at the door. The assumption that a mitzvah requires inner readiness as a condition for fulfillment does not lead to reform or to a revocation of the overall obligation to the commandments of the Torah. There are many mitzvot whose obligatory nature I understand very well as it applies to someone in a historical situation or cultural condition or a phase of spiritual development different from my own. For example, I realize that at a certain point in man's cultural development, which is paralleled by a certain phase in his spiritual development, the animal sacrifices are incumbent upon him as mitzvot. For that reason, in my own opinion, I am not canceling the force of these commandments out of the Torah when I state that I myself am not in that situation or that state of corresponding spiritual development. Therefore, even if those commandments were in force at the present time, from the point of view of external circumstances, I would not regard myself as obligated to observe them. For me, in keeping with the inner set of my life, they would achieve an end which would be the opposite of their original intention as it is specified in the Torah.

As an aside, it is proper to mention here that these words would be acceptable to many Jews who label themselves as Orthodox, though it might be doubtful whether they would dare say them. At any rate, they are far from desiring those commandments or trying to bring about the conditions required for their performance. In that regard, at least, they are choosing their mitzvot. Be that as it may, in this instance, commandments that do not come our way are under discussion. Only a bold interpretation of them could direct them toward us and make them applicable; that is, their content would have to be given a different expression, one more suitable to our spiritual position, before we could regard ourselves as ready for them. And we might ask, parenthetically, whether a first step in this direction has not already been taken by the substitution of theoretical study of the sacrifices for the actual sacrifices themselves.

The above example has purposely been taken from among those mitzvot which have come down to us in a manner and formulation that create a clash between the commandments and other values which we regard ourselves as bound to uphold. But it seems to me that, despite the fact that we are accustomed to emphasize such clashes in our public debates, most of the commandments which the non-Orthodox Jew regards himself as unable to observe do not give birth to conflicts of this type. At the most one might say that they are "hard for him," because they are outside the accustomed and accepted way of life of most of the secular community. But even the difficulty they contain would not be felt in the slightest by the secularist Jew if he could find some meaning in them. The real problem, then, is that these mitzvot are simple devoid of significance for him—and a meaningless act automatically becomes a tiresome burden. Indeed, this fact of emptiness of meaning does not immediately change, even for someone who has reached a level of consciousness of obligation and is seeking to return to

92

Jewish life. Part of the commandments will seem charged with meaning for him, and he will embrace them. But another part will continue to appear to be stripped of all significance for him, and before that part he will stand confounded and despairing.

We repeat, this does not imply that these commandments will be regarded by him as if they are not mitzvot. For he can understand a spiritual condition to which they were directed, and he can even desire that condition. But he is still far from it. One can apply the words of the sages in regard to such commandments. They interpreted the verse "For it [the Torah] is not an empty thing for [Hebrew, literally, "from"] you" to mean that if there is emptiness, it is *from you*. That is, the dislocation in this instance is due to the fact that the person has not come to the mitzvah while regarding himself as bound by it. Of course, he can perform an act. He can observe all the prohibitions against work on the Sabbath, he can put on tefillin, and the like. But if he does so, he will be like an actor in his own eyes. Under these conditions, therefore, it seems to him that refraining from observing the mitzvah— out of hope for a development that will bring him closer to it—is not in a class with casting off the yoke of the Torah on his part. On the contrary, this is the only way in which a person who was not educated in the tradition can acknowledge a mitzvah and relate to it with dignity and acceptance of obligation. To be sure, this holds true only as long as it is his intention to continue taking on the obligation of the commandments of the Torah.

I wish now to recall an earlier judgment. In principle, the act of choice from the totality of the commandments is not the sole property of the non-Orthodox Jew. In principle, everyone who regards himself as bound to obey the commandments of the Torah acts in this manner. This is not meant to refer to human weakness, which can cause even the Jew who calls himself Orthodox to fail to perform all the mitzvot which he would like to fulfill. What is meant is the stirring of the desire from the direction of inner readiness for the mitzvah. Many positive commandments are incumbent upon every Jew at all times. He can fulfill only a part of them. So he chooses from among everything that is applicable to him day by day. He makes this choice in accordance with his own personal promptings in the general and particular circumstances he is in and in keeping with his inner inclinations. Some commandments are widely observed, while others remain forgotten or are postponed. Each period and every person has some commandments which are more precious than others—precious means nearer to our nature or inclinations and therefore more clearly significant.

But it is obvious that there is a fundamental difference between someone who is living fully within a social, familial, and personal setting that is shaped by the halakhah and someone who is not. More than a little, the inner preparation of every mitzvah depends on the continuum in which a person is living. It also depends upon the manner in which the total environment prepares the individual mitzvot it holds for us and puts a sense of belonging to the whole into each of them, even if the degree of emphasis is not equal for them all. Therefore, a selection which a person makes out of a fullness of a life led according to the halakhah cannot be compared to the choice made by one whose life is being led within a totality that has

94

been differently fashioned. The former includes most of his acts within the mitzvot. He is conscious of the totality and relates to it directly. Any commandment which he does not discharge, therefore, he does not put aside. Instead, through another mitzvah, he fulfills what he would have observed originally. The latter person includes only a small part of his actions within the mitzvot. He is not conscious of the totality and does not relate to it directly. Whatever he does not observe, therefore, he explicitly casts off. So even if one mitzvah draws him to another, he is still far, in observing the commandments that come his way, from what he would be performing with those which are still not prepared for him.

With this statement we come to the reason that there are so many commandments which the non-Orthodox Jew regards himself as unprepared for. They are cut off from the continuity of his life, a life which for the most part is being conducted in a different area. This, as we know, has not happened accidentally. It is the result of a definite historical reality. At the start of the modern age the institutions of the Jewish community disintegrated, and a large part of the Jewish people moved away from the traditional way of life. For that part, the chain of tradition was interrupted. Today the vast majority of the Jewish people have not received the Torah as it was passed on throughout earlier generations. There is only one way in which a tradition may be fruitfully carried on: the son receives it from his father, the pupil from his master—both in regard to learning and the continuity of a style of life.

I shall be more precise. The majority of the Jewish people have not received the Torah in its totality. This is because certain parts of it have come in a different context or with different degrees of intensity to anyone who is called a Jew. (It should not be necessary to mention that a total forgetting of the Torah is equivalent to a severing of the tie to the Jewish people.) In any case, the continuity has been broken and the total perfection marred. This is a fact which can be neither ignored nor done away with. It has been stamped upon the image of this generation and has determined its character. And this applies not only to those who have been alienated from the tradition, but also to those who are faithful to it. They too have been influenced by the change and have been radically altered by it.

Once we comprehend the reason for the alienation of most of the Jewish people of our time from the Torah and its commandments, we can also explain why part of the mitzvot seem close and understandable and inviting, while part remain alien. In most cases the reason is "biographical," though there are certainly broader historical reasons. At the start, a person is close only to those mitzvot which have come down to him from the past, through his parents and teachers or out of the environment in which he lives, out of a definite continuity of a way of life. Those commandments which his parents observed for various reasons—some personal, some social, some national—he still feels are sensible and near to him. Those which his parents neglected or rejected, he finds alien and meaningless. This, then, is not capricious. It is a reality which has its own logic. And, as we have said, that reality cannot be ignored without our being caught up in an arbitrary action.

Because we understand the logic of that reality,

however, we can propose a criterion of choice which will do no injury to the concept of tradition. On the contrary, this criterion sets itself firmly for tradition by applying its principles to the reality of a contemporary man who wants to return to the Jewish heritage. The standard is to let each person begin from the point at which tradition has come down to him. Let him keep whatever is suitable for himself according to his own training—and thus let him gradually try to seize a continuity and fullness of life in keeping with the mitzvah.

This is a personal criterion. In this matter it is impossible to give a clearly precise directive that would tell people: "Do this, don't do that," even though, after all is said and done, it will certainly be clear that the differences between Jews will not be great. They will find a common language and will be helped by one another. The only general rule is to perform what is right for you out of the Torah. Approach the totality from the place where you now stand. But it must be stressed over and over again that the aim must be toward the totality through study and deepening and through a gradual approach, going from the familiar mitzvot toward those that are related to them. For when a person seriously intends to observe mitzvot, he binds himself to the totality in one corner, and then he spreads his reach out wider and wider. From this point of view, a far-reaching difference becomes apparent between a man of our generation who is searching for a way to return, and the last generation. The last generation received a great deal from their parents. But because their inclination was outward, they passed on little to their children. The younger generation, when they try to return, have little which they received from their fathers. But because their inclination is inward, they can transmit more than they received.

I wish now to return to the comparison between the person who is seeking to return and the one who is permanently within the continuity of tradition. As has been said, the difference between them is not just one of the quantity of commandments which each is fulfilling. It is mainly a difference between a person who lives within the totality and someone who is outside it. One of its most important consequences is also that the one who stands within makes his choices according to an interpretation whose guidelines are based on a life-pattern that has been fashioned in accord with Jewish law, not in accord with a subjective postulate which is full of fragmentary and chance elements. For that reason he has the power to make halakhic decisions.

Someone who chooses his way back has nothing except what tradition places before him. He is unable to use it creatively. He measures himself by the halakhah. He can demand that it direct itself toward him; but he is unable to make decisions in keeping with it. This fact fixes a limit for the progress which he can make by his own powers. It has already been stated that the distance between the contemporary Jew and the halakhah originates not only in the fact that he has drifted away from it and is not prepared for it, but also because the halakhah has not touched him or prepared itself for him. How, then, can he come to shape a positive relationship with the totality in such a role? Only if, on his way back, he meets the bearers of halakhah coming out to meet him. Only if he finds them willing to coordinate Jewish law with the social and cultural reality in which we are living. Only if they will live within that reality and study it and prepare the needed halakhah for it, as the masters of Jewish law have done all through the ages.

One might expand at this point and discuss the problem as it arises from the side of that Judaism that is called Orthodox. Its unwillingness to behave within the reality of our generation, as the masters of halakhah have always conducted themselves within the reality of their generations in ages past, gives expression to the damage which has been done to Jewish law through the alienation of most of the Jewish people from the Torah. This lack of willingness has diminished the realm of application of the halakhah and slowed its growth. And while the halakhah retains its continuity, it is so limited a continuity that one cannot stand up straight inside it. But this is again a broad issue which cannot be dealt with in an offhand manner.

Let me summarize briefly. A man of our day who seeks to return to the tradition takes a single step and hopes that the door will be opened for him, so that he can pass through tall and straight. Otherwise he cannot enter. However, he can take the first step on his own. For there is authentic religious significance to a personal choice which is not capricious, but flows from the cultural reality in which he exists and turns toward the perfect wholeness in hope that his self-preparation for the mitzvah will be answered by a preparation of the mitzvah for him.

SUPPLEMENTARY NOTES

I

Only rarely in our generation do we encounter young people who have been reared in religious homes and then have drifted away from the religion in their mature years. But in our parents' generation this was the general rule. This general rule had an influence on the formation of such people's image of their world. It was part of their consciousness and affected the way in which they succeeded in imparting their heritage to their children. It is proper, therefore, for us to consider this image. We must examine it in order to be free of it, because it constitutes an obstacle. What typifies the world of the faith in the imagination of such people is that it is, as far as they are concerned, a juvenile world beyond which they have matured. To be sure, a child's world is a wonderful place—especially in the eyes of the adult who recalls it with nostalgia. It is a world of secure dependability. It is a world of absolute certainties. That's the trouble. The adult person stands outside the juvenile world looking in, for he has no way of going back. Adulthood cannot be forgotten.

But is the childish image of the world of faith a correct one? Is it complete? It is not my purpose to deny the importance of such a childhood experience in the development of the world of the believer. That is possibly a base without which the structure could not stand. But a religious person must also go through the crisis of maturing in the area of his faith. He must not remain a perpetual child religiously. If he does, and certainly many do, his faith is stunted and ludicrous, like any childishness that is carried beyond the

100

bounds of childhood. Indeed, the believer too is compelled to face up to the same questions which cause the alienated Jew to be as one on the outside looking in; but in facing them the religious person may have an expectation of a sort of revelation. And this is the source of the error. There is no way back to childhood. A mature person can return in penitence only if he makes his confrontation with the religious world of the adult.

Furthermore, one characteristic of the child's religiosity is the fact that, if the truth be told, he does not really grasp the first and primary concept of religion —the God concept. Nor does he understand properly the concept of mitzvah. Naturally, he has an image of God. But this is a copy of the image of the demanding, compelling father. He accepts the religious order of life, in which he was born and to which he is accustomed, as if it were a complete thing unto itself and could be no other way. That is the way things are. That is the way they have to be. It never occurs to him that they could be different. Thus he never asks by what power this order of life is required. For him, this is a fact which expresses only itself. And in such a role it can be quite simple and easy. Sin? Again, you cannot be sure until you fail to perform an act of atonement.

It is only natural for a person who has gotten away from the faith to long for this simple world of secure wholeness that makes its requirements by its own power. It is natural, too, for such a person to think that until he can go back to feeling that way, he cannot return to an observance of the commandments. But to me it seems doubtful that this simple view of the mitzvot is fundamentally correct. Does the system of mitzvot stand by its own power? Is it obvious? A person who has grown up in the faith may ask about the mitzvah and the manner in which it is commanded, about the reason for its being commanded, and about the significance of his being obligated under it. Of course, when he asks all these questions, the simple structure of the child totters; and nothing is obvious anymore. But only then can he understand the correct meaning of being under obligation to observe the commandments of God.

In the body of this chapter, the mitzvah was defined as a directive which we fulfill on the basis of recognition of the authority of the giver of the commandment, not out of compulsion. In a mitzvah, a person operates with free will and liberty, while the law not only requires him to act, but is forced upon him by certain sanctions. It must be said that when a person fulfills commandments because he is afraid of punishment or is hoping for a reward—whether from men in this world or from God in the next—he is not observing mitzvot, and his actions have no true religious significance. Only when he demonstrates his freedom in confrontation with the mitzvah does he stand in obedience before the law-giving God.

But only someone who has matured in his faith can fulfill a mitzvah in this manner. It is possible only for one who realizes that the religious order of life is not obvious and does not have validity on its own power or by the strength of its own routine. But Jewish law developed in circumstances where there was no distinction between the religious commandment, for which there were no sanctions in such a function, and the law of society, for which there were. Even today there are religious commandments which are en-

forced as laws by society—the ethical law which prevents one from injuring another person is one. Even
in such instances, however, one has the choice of
either obeying the directive on the basis of one's free
will and liberty—in which case one is fulfilling a social
or religious mitzvah—or refusing the command and
being forced to comply—in which case one is simply
bowing to the law. In such cases the difference between mitzvah and compulsion is merely one which
involves the state of a person's consciousness. But it is
a most meaningful difference for the person. Therefore it is absolutely proper to distinguish between
obedience to the law of society and fulfillment of the
mitzvah, even when there is no difference whatsoever
in the act itself.

II

The mitzvah, in its religious sense, stands on the sup-
position of the objective reality of the revelation. That
is, it stands in a position relative to the divine authority
before which we are in a state of obligation. When the
divine authority is replaced by a human element—
whether social or personal (for example, by conscience
or moral consciousness or national consciousness or
the like)—the religious sphere is totally blotted out. Of
course, even in this view, the divine command only
comes down to us through the mediation of human
agencies. These human elements must not represent
themselves as the source of the command, however,
for they would thus be assuming an authority which is
not theirs. They have only the status of intermediary.
They transmit and interpret what they have received;
their authority is confined to transmission and en-

ISRAEL AT THE CROSSROADS

largement on the basis of interpretation. This gives us
the reason to oppose both the Orthodox and the Reform approaches. The Orthodox give the human agencies the authority of coercion, in the name of the religion, in regard to actions which are in the category of
mitzvot. The Reform thinkers give the human agencies the authority to determine, purely on their own,
what is and what is not a divine commandment.

The basis of the tradition, though it is carried on by
man, is revelation. Tradition transmits revelation. Tradition perpetuates revelation. But man takes his position before the tradition as a free agent, not a subject
of compulsion. Social sanction for mitzvot, then,
means politization of religion. There are situations
and areas in which this is justified and even required
—from the political point of view. But there are also
circumstances in which it leads to utter perversion.
Theological sanction in behalf of the mitzvah—
heaven and hell, for example—is nothing more than a
transcription of the political into the realm of the religious. There are, apparently, circumstances in which
the coercive view seems acceptable. But those are the
circumstances of childhood. We must mature away
from them in order to arrive at an understanding of
the pure religious content of the mitzvah.

III

Finally, the grave question of political coercion for the
mitzvot frequently comes up. It is true that the commandments of the Torah are to be discharged by and
through the community. If the community breaks up,
the tradition is halted, and there will be no further
opportunity to observe the commandments. Since this

is the case, it is proper to examine how it can be possible to preserve the unity of the community without a certain amount of "religious coercion." It would seem that when the question is thus worded, one must respond that it is indeed impossible to preserve the community's unity without a certain measure of forced observance of the commandments through the intervention of human authority. But in replying in this manner, we must first of all be careful about the substitution for the religious interest of a political consideration which derives from it. Coercion is not implicit in the mitzvah itself. It is necessitated after our decision to respond by observing the commandment. Thus coercion flows from the human will. Logically, then, something which derives from human-political desire must be justified in a human-political fashion; for the religious command, in and of itself, does not represent a justification. And, of course, political justification for religious coercion is quite possible. In the framework of an aristocratic society such as that which was customary in the religious Jewish community of Europe, for example, the justification was based on the legitimate political mandates of a leadership that wished to observe the commandments. It was also based on the confidence which the Jewish community vested in that leadership. In the framework of a democratic society such as we are living in today in Israel, the justification can come only through general agreement by the agency of our elected officials.

If the mass of people wish to observe the commandments, it is proper to compel such observance to the extent that anyone refusing to comply would be disturbing the general public in carrying out its desire. This is, in my judgment, sufficient political justification to compel obedience to the traditional Jewish marriage laws, for example, as long as the official bodies representing the general public so will. But when the political framework of the religious community is broken, and attempts are made to force mitzvot on a nonreligious society on the basis of reliance on the *religious* validity of the commandments, then there could be no greater error than that in understanding the essence of the mitzvah. Nor could there be any more formidable obstacle that could be placed in the way of those who truly wish to return to Jewish tradition.

6
ZIONISM UNDER TESTING

The establishment of the State of Israel has caused confusion in the ideological evaluation of the various Zionist parties. This applies not only in determining orientation and function but also in the streams of political, social, and cultural activity in Israel and abroad. These parties, most of which had formulated their principles on the grounds of the Zionist ideology—though they had all added to it in keeping with their various particular social tendencies—now lost the basis on which they agreed or disagreed. Former programs that had been focuses of debate were now accomplished facts, which it made no sense to continue thrashing over. Means, over which battles had been waged, had already attained their ends. There remained, then, a narrow area of tactical disagreement and conflicts of interest among leaderships and establishments. This could not provide a basis for ideological confrontation, or even genuine political confrontation. It seemed that the State had exhausted everyone's emotional drives by furnishing the desired end product, and the Zionist parties went on existing only by the waning power of routine.

How can that scene be explained? The most widespread evaluation placed before us is that of the "natural" phenomenon of a movement which has accomplished its goal, or at least succeeded in achieving it to a recognizable extent. The State had taken over the functions of the Zionist movement and left it without a real role. But within the confines of the State we were confronted with both external and internal conditions which did not permit us choices among various paths. Instead, our way was determined by the imperatives of absorption of immigration, development of Israel's economy, and reinforcement of our security position under political siege. We were forced to conduct a policy, the sole end of which was to give Israel a firm base and secure its survival. It is natural that very little room was left for tactical divergences, and none for approaches that conflicted in principle.

This description of the prevailing situation, though it appears rather reasonable at first glance, nevertheless requires a more exacting examination. Are we really only dealing with a crisis of accomplishment, or should the crisis also be extended to include what Zionism did *not* accomplish? Perhaps there was something in Zionism's overall orientation which manifested itself as erroneous precisely after the Zionist movement's greatest achievement. And from this point we may ask again whether Zionism solved the problems with which it struggled. Does it have the ability to propose an answer to the problems that have not yet been solved?

As we know, Zionism offered a solution to both the Jewish problem and the problem of Judaism. For those who struggled for its realization, it did indeed solve them—but not in the manner they had believed it would. They had thought in terms of a "final" solution

108

—the liquidation of the Diaspora, or at least the prevention of the dangers of destruction and assimilation in the Diaspora. In practice, Zionism did not liquidate the Galut even after the establishment of Israel. Moreover, it did not even remove the peril of assimilation. If it did solve a problem, it was because Zionism preserved the people in spite of the dangers, not because it ended them. It did not liquidate the Exile, but it did provide an outlet for protest against Diaspora life. Zionism did not overcome the process of assimilation. But it did bind large sections of the Jewish people to Judaism by offering them an area of Jewish political activity.

Of course, a solution which does not end the problem only creates a new situation that is but a variation of the previous condition. The variation is likely to alleviate some problems and make others more grave. But the earlier solution is no longer able to give answers to the questions that have been raised in altered form in the new variation. And this is the source of the crisis which is troubling the Zionist movement today. It is not the movement's accomplishments which have caused it. Nor has it been brought about by the fact that the instrumentalities of the State are in a position to fulfill Zionism's functions more efficiently. Quite the opposite. All the problems which Zionism had thought to solve have risen up afresh after the historical situation has thoroughly changed. Naturally, the very alteration of the historical situation represents an important accomplishment. And in a number of senses, this is a decisive achievement for which the Zionist movement is to be thanked. But its great crisis has its source in two facts. (1) It can no longer propose the same answers to the same questions. (2) Some of the questions have been made even more grave, to a great extent, by Zionism itself.

This assumption requires us to reexamine Zionism's solutions in the three important areas where it carried on its struggle: (1) the relationship of the modern Jew to the Jewish cultural heritage and the Jewish religion —an area which involves the problem of the continuity of Judaism as a unique and separate spiritual phenomenon; (2) the relationship of the Jewish people to the Diaspora; and (3) political, social, and cultural relations between Israel and the nations.

Zionism offered one single answer to all three questions: the creation of a national home for the Jewish people in the land of Israel. That would guarantee the continuation of original cultural creativity. In the national home, all the distortions of the Exile would be corrected. And through the self-sufficiency of the national home, the tragic tension between Israel and the nations would finally evaporate.

Now that the State has been established, have all these things happened? Or have all the focal points of danger perhaps been inflamed again within and around about Israel?

The Tie to Jewish Tradition

The establishment of the State of Israel was made possible by the tragic sharpening of the "Jewish problem" after World War II. But Zionism was born, paradoxically, as a result of the tragic sharpening of the "problem of Judaism." It was—though not always in its own sight, and never with utter thoroughness—a movement of "return" to Judaism from the paths of alienation and assimilation which had opened up in modern times. For West European Jewry, Zionism

110

was mainly a return from assimilation. For East European Jewry (with the exception of religious Zionism, which must be considered separately) it was a return from Enlightenment-type criticism and adherence to various political movements which were outside the realm of Judaism. In both cases, this was a paradoxical effort to perpetuate Judaism outside the circle of its traditional values, in the form of a dialectic continuation of those values. The characteristic dualism of Zionism's relations to the sources of Judaism derives from this.

Zionism appeared as a movement of revolt against the orientation of an ancient tradition—in order to save that very tradition. And Zionism ended up caught inextricably between its conflicting drives. It shot back and forth between the denial which held an affirmation and the affirmation which contained a denial. The only possibility of working to save what could be rescued of the tradition without forgoing the revolt was to put off a frontal conflict with the tradition and its culture. The Zionist movement found ways to coexist in Jewry with the problem and despite the problem. But postponing the confrontation did not always lead to a cancellation of the reality of the problem. Sometimes it worsened it many times over.

The founder and most distinguished representative of West European Zionism, Herzl, defined Zionism as a road back to Judaism. But what did he mean by that statement? It appears that the act of political organization for a solution of the Jewish problem gave him full satisfaction. He did not ask about the content of a philosophy, and he was certainly not seeking a way of life. His one and only goal was the creation of a sepa-

111

rate and independent political structure in which Jews would be able to live an undisturbed secular-European cultural life. He surely envisioned a cultural uniqueness for the Jewish State. But by this he meant its "idealism," that is, its anticipated success in achieving the realization of principles drawn from Western culture.

According to Herzl's thinking, then, the tie to Judaism has national significance. Political and social conclusions have to be drawn from it. But it requires no cultural or religious conclusions whatsoever. This represented a total ignoring of the problem of Judaism as a spiritual problem. It was a disregard that apparently was characteristic of West European Zionism in general. It is no wonder, then, that the most forceful criticism of Zionism—and today we may confess openly that it was a criticism which contained more than a kernel of truth—came from within West European Orthodoxy.

The position of East European Zionism, particularly that of the pioneering labor movement, was not far from the stand of Western Zionism ideologically. But from a psychological point of view, the tension (which was expressed in its belles lettres) was incomparably greater. Those educated in the traditional Jewish school system, and those who had been raised in homes where Jewish faith and tradition were still being carried on, were consciously or unconsciously searching in their Zionism for relief from the pain of separation from the spiritual world in which they had been reared. Zionism's claim that it offered personal fulfillment was not only the result of the distress which was harsher in the East than it was in the West. It was the product of a grass-roots Judaism for which Zionism

112

was a substitute in conviction and way of life. It flowed from the most intimate sources of Jewish literature. Such, at any rate, was the real reason for the opposition on the part of East European Zionists to the Uganda program and their stubborn adherence to Palestine—even though their position did not always follow logically from the official ideology which was current among them.

Even when it conflicted with his proclaimed views, the East European Zionist desired not only political independence, but also the adaptation of the content of a heritage symbolized by Eretz Israel. Going back to the homeland meant returning to the Holy Land, the land of the Bible and prophets. Doing without Palestine, however, was tantamount to forgoing the last thread which tied the Jew who had come from a traditional background to the heritage of his fathers. It was not possible to accept this act of separation without perverting the spiritual significance of Zionism as a movement of return.

But a dualism was intrinsic to the very nature of the Zionism movement. It had an involuntary need for abstract concepts and organizational methods which were not only borrowed from outside Judaism, but even emanated from those very processes which had placed the continuity of Jewish tradition in doubt. Thus even in eastern Europe, Zionism was no more than an experiment in the paradoxical business of living as a Jew—outside of Judaism.

Consider, for example, the writings of Y. H. Brenner. They offer an extreme model, the exceptional nature of which is in itself instructive. On the surface his stories and articles are laden with cutting criticism of Judaism. Zionism is, for him, liberation from the

113

weight of a despised and backbreaking inheritance. Through the Zionist movement, he is striving for a Jewish life freed from the burden of the past. But even those of his contemporaries who debated with him recognized that his words were not to be taken literally. His exaggerated criticism was merely the fruit of an injured love. It drew sustenance from a tragic life experience which involved rebellion against the Jewish destiny. It therefore contained an element of justice. But that element was not present in the exposed face of his criticism of Judaism. It was to be found, rather, in the sensation within, a sensation of revolt from which reverberated an incomparable proclamation of faith.

This, it would seem, is a considered and correct evaluation which must be reemphasized even in regard to those who want to take Brenner at face value, as well as in refutation of those who would smear him with the sins of extremism and bad judgment. But no matter how right this estimate may be, it only serves to bear witness to a serious spiritual labyrinth. The damaged love which has been transposed into burning hatred testifies to the incongruity between the secular philosophy of Brenner the Zionist, who can never reconcile himself to the Jewish fate because it is meaningless to him, and his awareness of belonging to the cultural environment, which shaped his whole personality to the point where he is unable to free himself of his cultural past. In his hatred of Judaism, Brenner hated himself. This is his justification, but it is also his tragedy. He was unable to affirm his existence consciously.

The same applies as well to Brenner's opponents, to A. D. Gordon and Joseph Vitkin, for example. However, in their simpler and more harmonious minds, love was not replaced by hate. But neither was their highly abstract love able to justify itself properly within their philosophies of life. They lived with it under the pressure of intellectual distress. What Vitkin wrote (in *Ketavim* [Hebrew], p. 90) on the subject of the election and eternity of Israel is especially characteristic. He declared: "As much as we sneer at it, and are sometimes embarrassed by it, it fills our hearts; and it is what gives us the strength to live and fight for life! Take this awareness away from us, and we are dead." But why do "we sneer at" this concept and why are we even "sometimes embarrassed by it"? For no other reason than that the concept was unjustifiable within the context of the view of Vitkin the Zionist, who had worked out a Western-secular philosophy for himself. In his opinion, ideas that grow out of the mystery of Jewish faith are pulsating through Zionism. They are the source of its strength to struggle and achieve its goals. But Zionism itself is unable to give them full expression in its ideational substructure.

What, then, is the way out? Postponement. Postponement's most typical advocate is A.D. Gordon. Every people has its own unique creative spirit. The Jewish people also has its own authentic spirit. It is recognizable in Jewish creativity in every age. The Exile prevents the free expression of Jewish originality, and the goal of Zionism is to remove that obstacle. Zionism prepares the ground without having to foresee the nature of the crop that would someday spring from it. Give the Jewish people an independent existence and an independent and unique Jewish creation would automatically take shape. It would be that creativity which would determine the Judaism and

115

Jewishness of every Jew, without his being consciously required to take forethought about the fixed values of his past.

Indeed, slipping out of the obligation to specific values without rejecting the original spirit of the Jewish people was what made it possible for Gordon and his followers to devote themselves to the realization of Zionism without solving the problem itself. This was what gave the Jewish pioneer who had come to Palestine the license to affirm his Judaism and Jewishness as they stood—with the full burden of European culture which he had taken on, and with the gap which had been opened between his thinking and actions and those of the culture of his fathers.

Of course, this does not mean that it was a return devoid of significance. When all is said and done, the halutz brought along a weighty cargo in the form of his inheritance of Jewish education and destiny. But an automatic confirmation of belonging, without a requirement toward the well-defined content of a tradition by which a person fulfills his Jewishness in his daily way of life, was not without its effects. Ultimately, with no pangs of conscience, one dislocated a link in the chain of a tradition that had been carried on from generation to generation. We are confronted with a Jewish community which received a bequest and felt no obligation to pass it on to those who came after. That community drew sustenance from a treasure with whose values it could not consciously identify. For that community, the treasure was only a factor which stimulated people to love and devotion. But love and devotion, be they ever so great, cannot comprise a legacy for the next generation unless there is a conscious identification with values and ways of life.

The generation of the fathers was therefore doomed to secure the continued existence of the Jewish people without being able to secure the continued influence of the spiritual sources by virtue of which it had accomplished its work.

Zionism, then, never had a solution to the problem of Judaism. It ignored that question—and in this regard its critics were correct. It was, of course, able to free spiritual forces which made it possible to disregard this fact. Thus Zionism was able to save the Jewish loyalty of many Jews who were on the brink of assimilation. But the closer the establishment of the State drew, the more dangerous this neglect became. A new generation soon arose to pose the question in a new way. Zionism could only respond to it by explaining the increasing gravity of the problem, but the movement was unable to give an answer to it. The youth that grew up in Palestine in the lap of Zionism accepted the fact of their Jewishness without ever having received the content of the Jewish heritage. The same was no less true of young people in the Diaspora whose parents had clung to Judaism by way of Zionism. Palestinian youth were raised in a culture that had been swept clean and around which there remained only the walls of a solid political structure. Diaspora youth experienced a faltering framework of questionable national affiliation.

The way in which the question arose again was new. We now had a generation with no direct basis in the tradition of its ancestors. And this was the case not only in regard to the tradition's content and the way of life it represented, but also in reference to the deposits of memory which comprise the essential strata of individual experience and build the personality. To affirm one's Judaism now, as it stood, meant to affirm a nationalism emptied of all cultural content. This was a nationalism devoid of any ability to tie itself to the past or serve as a connecting link between the individual Jew and the future. Admittedly, this is neither an intellectual crisis nor a rebellion. The problem is raised not out of the need to choose between two cultures, but because of cultural emptiness on both sides equally. Should he borrow from European culture? He—at least the Palestinian youth—had no direct contact with its sources. Should he return to the culture of his fathers? But the continuity of practice of a way of life, by which alone one may acquire a genuine grasp of Jewish tradition, had been interrupted.

A clear witness to this development is the approach of Palestinian-born young people to a Zionism which, for them, was bracketed between a pair of quotation marks. What did this approach mean? Anyone who knows the issues up close knows that this was no "revolt" or even criticism of the goals of Zionism and its methods of achieving them. Their interest in Zionism did not even go that far. It was, simply, an expression of lack of concern for ideas that had grown to be so routine. The validity of those ideas was assumed as a postulate. But to return to them would have been regarded as a useless effort. Zionism was right. Fine. But it was an answer to someone else's question. This generation was no longer asking that question. It had its own questions, to which Zionism gave no answers. Therefore, Zionism was irrelevant.

Why was Zionism not relevant for them? Because the national and social goal, the achievement of which demanded self-sacrifice for the creation of a vast work, appeared to the native-born youth as an objective *to-*

ward which one lived. But it did not impart meaning to a person's life while it was being lived. Such meaning, which can be attained solely within the daily contact between one person and another and between a person and himself, could not be derived from Zionism. Nor could it impart significance to the life of a Jew who was not born in the Diaspora and for whom the concept of the rejection of the Galut was not a matter of personal experience. Meaning of that order can emanate solely from a cultural tradition. Therefore only one who had directly benefited from the cultural tradition of the Judaism of the Diaspora, from that Judaism which nurtured Zionism, could have experienced Zionism while living toward it. For the native youth, Zionism was merely an ideology. And that, like any ideology, was too thin to provide an outlet for an individual's emotions or to serve adequately as a vehicle for his thoughts or for his public actions. This is why Zionism became irrelevant.

(Today the thoughts of the foregoing paragraph appear to me to be subject to revision; see the next chapter, "A Time of Returning.")

However, there was more to it than this. It was the Zionist project which brought about the situation that raised the questions of the youth. The years of Zionist education were not directed toward imparting cultural values to the students. That education pictured the creation of such values as the automatic outcome of the realization of the work of Zionism. Zionist education also frequently was based on the concept of Galut negativism, in both the political and cultural meaning of the term. The cultural emptiness, together with the rejection of the Diaspora, served to sever the traditional continuity of Jewish culture. That

119

is, Zionism took a position, before the young generation in Israel, not of a connecting link, but of an open link dangling weakly at the end of a chain without acting as an attachment for anything to follow.

The younger generation were asking the question of the spiritual meaning of their existence. Thus they were raising anew the problem of Judaism. Actually, this is the consummate question for the Jewish people of today. Is there any value in carrying on the struggle for the survival of a people which has lost its cultural uniqueness? And is there any chance for the success of such a struggle? Is it enough for the Jewish people to have a state—"like all the nations?"

Zionism, by ignoring these questions, greatly increased their seriousness. Now as they confront us, in the very midst of a battle to maintain the greatest of Zionism's achievements, Zionism is no longer able to propose an answer to them.

(Today the relationship between Judaism and Zionism seems different. But it is certain that a substantive tie to Judaism and a Jewish education, insofar as possible, are prerequisites for inculcating Zionist consciousness into the heart of the rising generation in Israel. Today, it seems to me, a knowledge of Zionism can be a lever by which the student can be brought close to Judaism.)

Homeland and Diaspora

Zionism, then, gave its answer to the question of Judaism in an indirect, rather than a direct, manner. Correcting what was wrong with the life of the Jewish people would assure the renewal of its spiritual creativity. Therefore Zionism omitted a detailed discussion on this issue. The Zionist movement preferred

120

to stress the two most outstanding aspects of the wrong which was being criticized by the Zionists. First, the Diaspora offered an unsatisfactory social, economic, and political existence for the Jew. Second was the tense relationship between Jewry and the non-Jewish world which prevailed in the Diaspora. On these two subjects, Zionism specified rigid rules and outlined clear programs.

The positive definition of Zionism is a hope for the establishment of a national home in Palestine for the Jewish people. But the definition that means the most in the history of Jewish culture is one that describes Zionism as an active, all-embracing rejection of the Galut. This includes existence in the Exile, which is negated because of the misery and danger of destruction it entailed. And it involves, no less, the negation of the life that was shaped in the Exile, because of the economic and social distortion, as well as the "degeneracy" in spiritual creativity it brought about. Zionism did not just reject the Galut as a historic condition that had been forced on the Jewish people against its will and to its detriment. Zionism also negated the Galut features in the Jewish character. It rejected Jewry's very existence as an exile people. It sought to bring about a change in the Jewish spiritual being no less than it aimed at altering the people's political, social, and economic condition.

Indeed, this negation contained much more spiritual quality than could have been held by the positive Zionist ideology. Incidentally, deep within it lay a confrontation with strata of experience that are primal in the makeup of the "secular" Jew. It is by understanding the negation of the Galut that we can explain the fact that Zionism as life experience was in some ways preferable to Zionism as nationalist thought-system or as political program. This negation served as a focus for emotional and intellectual activity, even though its ideological expression was limited to the point of poverty. This is the source of Zionism's immense influence. It was this which made Zionism the only expression of spiritual life for a large portion of the Jewish people. And this is true not just for the halutz, who drew a consistent conclusion and went to Palestine in order to experience Zionist fulfillment. It also applies to the vast majority which remained in the Galut and found an outlet in identifying with Zionism's aims, participating in its organization, and doing its work in the community.

However, this spiritual activity of rejection of the Galut involved a confrontation with the Jewish heritage which each Zionist had received in accordance with his own level of Jewish education and the environment from which he had come. At the heart of this negation lay the dualism of the Zionist's relationship to the Galut. This is a dualism which is nurtured by the complex attitude of the secularist Jew toward Jewish tradition. In the one case, he sought to perpetuate Jewish life outside the circle of Jewish life. And in the other instance, he was trying to remove the Jewish people from the Galut experience by using the powers of the Galut and working within its confines. He wanted to negate it, and thereby automatically facilitate its perpetuation.

This dualistic approach to the Diaspora was stamped on the actions of the Zionist movement. It made itself visible in conceptual difficulties from which Zionism labored in vain to escape. Finally it

122

received unconcealed prominence in several formulations of Zionism. This is especially clear, though in a
simplistic form, in the political orientation of West
European Zionism. This phase of the movement was
not generally marked by multidimensionality. The
desire to establish the Jewish national home in keeping with the law of the nations and by means of political negotiation derived more from the psychological
need of Western Jewry—which was on the brink of
assimilation—than it did from a realistic consideration
of given facts and potentialities. Political activity itself
gave direction and purpose to a separate national organization. And that organization itself, existing side
by side with other organizations, was sufficient justification for the continuation of life in the Galut—even
if all the activity did not immediately achieve its ends.
The very chance of success offered great relief, because the activity which voiced the rejection of Exile
life already contained the possibility of justifying a
continuation of that life. Therefore, the longing to
serve as a pioneer in rebuilding the Jewish homeland
—and thereby turn Zionist theory into practice—was
not felt with full force in the West.

East European Jewry's relationship to Zionism was
much more complicated in this respect. The suffering
was many times worse, and the longing infinitely
stronger. But even in this case, the dualism showed
itself in full force. Indeed, the intent here is not to
point at the majority of the members of the Hoveve
Zion—those lovers of Zion at a distance—who preferred to work for Eretz Israel in their countries of
residence. They made their Zionism into an intellectual support for their permanent lives in the Exile. A
movement is not to be judged by the actions of a

majority of its members who are unable to be consistent for many reasons, not all of which should be made light of. It must be judged by the paths of activity to which it adheres, even if its accomplishments are isolated.

Therefore, we may see the most consistent ideological response of Zionism in eastern Europe in the halutz movement. Even that was not free of dualism. The pioneer who went to Palestine and rebelled against the Galut took its heritage with him. If he had not been educated in it, it is doubtful whether he would have reached such a high level of consistency in his realization of Zionism. From the point of view of his experience, then, he was tied to the Diaspora, and this tie continued for him, even in Palestine. This was true in both his political and communal work. Palestine could not have been built up except with the power of a strong Diaspora that was possessed of national pride, as well as spiritual—and material—riches. It required a Diaspora with sufficient strength to struggle for its own salvation. We can state quite simply that the very existence of the Palestinian work depended, at least during the years of contruction, on the presence of a powerful and solidly based Galut. It was inevitable, then, that Zionism should justify its reinforcement of the Diaspora, if only as a temporary measure, even while the Zionist movement was proclaiming a doctrine of Galut negativism.

How was this to be done? The halutz movement found the practical way, though it never made a theoretical admission of the fact. It cultivated firm ties between Palestine and the Diaspora by sending out emissaries, aiding Jewish education in the youth movements and schools, engaging in organizational

activity within the institutions of the Zionist movement, and doing other work of this nature. All this was
—and we may allow ourselves the use of the term,
even though it was far from the ideological language
of Labor Zionism—a practical implementation of the
concept of the "spiritual center." Perhaps this was the
only possible form of realization for that idea. During
that period, as a matter of fact, Palestine served as the
spiritual center of the Diaspora. It poured out into the
Galut a sense of national pride, security and hope, as
well as a literature, an ideology, and the knowledge of
a way of life. All this strengthened and sustained the
Jewish communities abroad.

We have mentioned the concept which explicitly
expressed Zionism's ambiguous attitude toward the
Galut—the idea of a spiritual center. Halutz Zionism,
as we have said, rejected this concept. The pioneering
phase of the movement drew its followers' devotion
largely from its aspiration for total achievement, while
Ahad Ha-am's doctrine was based on disbelief in the
possibility of a total achievement. But in spite of this,
even the pioneering movement came to the doorstep
of that program. Only by virtue of Labor Zionism's
extremism was it possible to disregard it during the
first phases of Zionist realization. Palestine was intended to lay the foundation for the full solution of the
Jewish problem, no less. Of course, if such a solution
could have been carried out in short order, it is possible that the ambivalent relationship of halutz Zionism
to the Galut would have been explained away as the
inevitable by-product of a transition period, during
which the Diaspora would have gradually disappeared as Palestine was built up.

But a complete solution was impossible. This fact became evident with the establishment of the State of Israel. At the same time, it became obvious that the State was unable to survive without the continuous help of the Diaspora. It was then that the tendency to compromise with the concept of a spiritual center won out. It was made into a sort of official program to which everyone paid homage. Even now, after the Six-Day War, there is no fundamental change in this situation, though the demand for *aliyah* has increased in strength.

What, then, is the significance of the spiritual center concept? It is explicitly stated by Ahad Ha-am. The intention is to build up the land of Israel in order to preserve, not to liquidate, the Diaspora. Israel is to create an authentic Jewish culture from which every Jew can draw sustenance, even if he is not a party to its creation. From that culture he will get literature, art, science, and thought—all stamped with the seal of an original creative Jewish spirit. In that culture he will see an unquestionable sign of the existence of a Jewish nation. Through that culture he will sense his affiliation with a community that has a full national life. This will also make him better understood by his non-Jewish neighbor. Ahad Ha-am believed that in this manner assimilation would be halted, and that the Jew would be able to take part in the life of his surroundings. Yet Ahad Ha-am's belief in the permanent existence of the Diaspora does not mean that he failed to share in the doctrine of the negation of the Galut. That doctrine was characteristic of all the factions of Zionism. On the contrary, his evaluation of the Galut was no less dark than that of its most extreme critics. He was aware of the social and economic destruction of the masses of Jewry, and he was even more sensitive to their spiritual annihilation. But once he realized that it was not possible to liquidate the Diaspora, he searched for a way in which a "normal" Galut could be established. That is, he sought for a practical means of removing the feeling of exile from the Diaspora. The spiritual center in Palestine, in which a normal Jewish society would be created, would also relieve the abnormal tension on the circumference.

Thus Zionism backed down from its total negation of the Galut and took a position whereby Palestine was to be built up as a surety for the continued survival of the Diaspora, while the Diaspora was to be maintained as a guarantee for the existence of the State. With the establishment of Israel, the spiritual center concept became the program of the Zionist movement. But there was an irony in all this that laid bare the paradox contained by Zionism. The spiritual center concept never served as a common basis for the most active sections of the movement throughout the time it was being implemented by them and while it had some significance. It was made into an inseparable part of Zionist ideology only when that significance began to drain away.

During the years of struggle for the soil of Palestine and the creation of the Jewish community there, the land of Israel was, as has been stated, a center for the Diaspora in practice, if not in theory. Through Palestine, broad strata of the Jewish people were tied in to Jewishness. Because of Palestine, they lived Jewish lives and involved themselves in Jewish activity. This was the only way in which the homeland could constitute a center for the Galut. It could not serve as a "producing" center for a "consuming" circumference. Nor could the Diaspora operate as an entity dispensing charity to a Jewish community fighting for its life in Palestine. But the relationship had to be one of a Galut which was directly building the homeland while regarding the Yishuv gathering there as its representative, fulfilling its mission.

Palestine remained the spiritual center for the Diaspora as long as the Jewish communities abroad had an active and direct role in the building of the country; as long as the Jewish pioneer was a child of the Galut and still carried its culture in him; as long as he was tied to it by his memories and family and community relationships; and, on the other hand, as long as the Diaspora was needed for organizational, economic, political, and educational efforts which directly influenced the Yishuv. Palestine was an area of creative activity which touched the personal life of every Zionist abroad. And creative activity is the only means through which a person can lead a spiritual life.

With the establishment of the State of Israel, this situation was fundamentally altered. It is true that the Yishuv still depended on the activity of the Diaspora. Of course, Israel still had a considerable influence on Jews overseas. But the land of Israel no longer constituted a field of direct activity for the Diaspora. Such a relationship appeared impossible. This was true, first of all, because the State of Israel defined itself as a separate political entity with its own institutions. It brooked no outside interference. Second, time had allowed the immigrants to strike roots in the land. A generation of native sons had been born, and their way of life was strange to the Diaspora. Thus the personal and social tie to the Galut was cut. Third, Diaspora Jews themselves did not desire to be directly responsible for the actions of a state in which they themselves were not citizens, even if the State of Israel had agreed to such a situation. (Now, after the Six-Day War, of course, the opportunity has been offered to renew the former healthy condition. But this depends more than a little on the willingness of the State to open itself to the activity of Jews abroad.)

But once Israel was created, the State constituted an independent unit. When it was spoken of as a spiritual center, the term was used in the meaning given it by Ahad Ha-am. In his view, Jews would live at a distance from it and bask in the light of Eretz Israel. The very existence of the State would increase their stature. From it, they would draw spiritual nourishment, including literature, art, and a social way of life. In a word, Israel would pour a constant stream of Jewish creativity into the bottomless pit of a receptive Diaspora that had nothing of its own to offer.

But in this meaning, the spiritual center concept in Ahad Ha-am's formulation was and is no more than an unsuccessful attempt to squirm out of a troublesome question which has cast doubt on Zionism as a complete solution to either the Jewish problem or the problem of Judaism. An Israel which is not an anvil for the creativity of the Diaspora cannot be a "spiritual center." Consumerism cannot, by any manner or means, be a way of participating in spiritual life. If the Diaspora does not create its own cultural works, it will take part in the creativity of the nations among which it exists, and it will identify with them. No educational activity proceeding from Israel can ever prevent the assimilation that will result from this process. Such activity will be helpless if for no other reason than that it will have nothing on which to base itself.

Clearly, one ought not to underestimate the importance of the role which the State plays in the life of the Jewish people. It constitutes a guarantee for the people's continuation and carries out the adjustment required to adapt the Jewish people to the political conditions of our times. It offers a secure refuge to those Jewish communities whose position may be insecure. It characterizes the Jewish people in the area of international politics. It assures, if only in one place, the survival of a Jewish society which will display all the characteristics of an independent nation. There is also, certainly, truth in the claim that the existence of the Jewish State provides a feeling of pride and security in the heart of the Jews of the Diaspora. And it is even correct to state that the opportunities for the emergence of authentic Jewish creativity are very great in Israel, even if they are not guaranteed.

But all these facts cannot make Israel into a spiritual center. They merely give the State a uniquely vital role in assuring the preservation of the Jewish people. In the next chapter we shall see how Israel's function in the life of the Diaspora has changed since the Six-Day War. But one must doubt the desirability of working for a situation in which the Diaspora would require Israeli creativity to the point of utter dependence—because that would mean the "liberation" of the Diaspora from independent creative efforts. And that would mean "freeing" the world's Jews for assimilation. So many people today are talking about Israel as a spiritual center without even trying to designate the means by which the State is to fulfill that function. We may well ask: How do you export culture? And what culture do we mean? And how can the Diaspora be in need of it? All this only goes to show that we are confronted with an attempt to put off by vagueness a troublesome question for which there is no answer: Can Zionism still be regarded as the sole solution to the Jewish problem even after it has become clear beyond the least doubt that for a long time to come the Jewish people will continue living with the overwhelming part of its population in the Galut? The concept of the spiritual center offers no answer. It only enables us to go on clinging to the same old shibboleths.

Here, too, we may summarize. Zionism provided an outlet for protest against Galut existence and its perils. But it did not do this by inventing a means to liquidate the problem or to correct old wrongs. Instead, it opened up a stream of activity for the Jew. The very act of *striving* for the reconstruction of the national home gave release to the Galut's feeling of rejection. But when the reconstruction reached the level of political definition and the Yishuv cut the umbilical cord that tied it to the Diaspora, it became evident that the problem had come to life in full force a second time, for Israelis as well as Jews in other lands. How can stability, freedom, and creative power be imparted to the Diaspora? How can you preclude the dangers and wrongs of the Galut—without destroying the basis of its existence? How can the growth of alienation among the various interdependent segments of the Jewish people be prevented? This is the way in which the problem of the relationship between homeland and Diaspora comes up again. But Zionism, having won its victory and thereby raising the question, is no longer able to offer a solution.

131

(Today, however, after the Six-Day War, it seems that the Zionist movement may be able to provide a reply, though not in the classic manner. This will be discussed in the next chapter.)

Israel and the Nations

The goal of repairing the distortions of the Diaspora by way of a return to a Jewish state was also the result of a reevaluation of traditional values in terms alien to the tradition. Of course, it never occurred to any Jewish thinker to picture the Galut as a satisfactory condition. Even those who interpreted it as a necessity for the fulfillment of the mission of Israel regarded it as the product of a catastrophe. The Exile was a symbol of the incompleteness of the creation, and the chosen people was also the chosen sacrifice. But this type of Galut negativism was not accompanied by the desire to improve the destiny of the Jewish people or to reform its way of life in accordance with a norm dictated from without. Exile was the tragic norm of a Jewish history, the events of which were carried through as something happening between a people and its God. It was an authentic revelation of the chosen people's state of being. As such, one could be reconciled to it on a temporary basis.

In contrast, Zionist thought saw the Exile purely as an evil occurrence, a meaningless deviation from the natural course. Zionism made its critique of Jewish history on the basis of the secularistic concepts of the nations of Europe. It sought to appear normal to them on their own model.

Zionism's goal of obliterating the Diaspora in order to adjust itself to other peoples' manner of existence also includes the fundamental objective of balancing the external tension between the Jew and his sur-roundings. When the Jewish people returned to its land, it would show its capacity in its own state and become a nation like all the other nations. The barri-ers walling it off would finally fall. It would no longer need the protective fences of Jewish law which serve to interrupt open social intercourse between Jews and Gentiles. Such legal devices could be dispensed with, since the Jew's separate national existence would no longer be in doubt and he would no longer be a stranger to his surroundings. He would relate to his environment exactly like a member of any other peo-ple. A common language among equals would be brought into being. And thus a balance would be es-tablished between Israel and the nations.

But in this matter, too, Zionism was thrust into a position that was loaded with inner contradictions, from the point of view both of the emotions that were being expressed and the reality that was being created. The aspiration of the modern Jew for normal-ization of relations with his environment was the di-rect result of the sharpening enmity toward the Jew-ish people. But while this sharpening gave rise to a tendency to close oneself off within the confines of an independent Jewish society that paralleled the lines of the hostile environment, it also stirred feelings of strong opposition to that hideous, malevolent environ-ment. It seemed that, against his own will, the Jew caught up in Zionism became aware once more of the ethical uniqueness and the destiny contained within the special fate of his people. Thus, as much as Zionism expressed a desire to be like all the rest of the nations, it also voiced an angry protest against those nations. It is not surprising that we should discover the buds of a paradoxical resurrection of the doctrine of election in Zionist thought. And this despite the fact that the concept of Jewish chosenness had no more severe critics than the Zionists.

It was obvious that opposition to the environment would eventually pass away as the special sensibility of a transition period, if it was possible to establish soon a condition for the Jewish people parallel to that of other nations. However, the Zionist movement perpetuated it by the very process by which the national home was established in Palestine. The Jew who left Europe as one leaves an exile came into conflict in his own land with the Arab inhabitant. At the same time, in many of the countries of Europe and America, a relaxation of tension and even a hastening of integration of the Jew into the environment were under way. Thus it turned out that precisely in the place where, according to the Zionist vision, increased hostility was to be anticipated, a distinct easing of hostility occurred—to the point where there was danger of assimilation. And at the same time, in the place where a weakening of tension had been predicted, relationships became charged with bitterness and enmity, the causes and results of which were different from, but no less intense than, what had gone before.

Zionism's approach to the Arab problem—and it was something that could not be avoided—was not one of frontal, open engagement. The moral dilemma was there from the start. At no time did a smooth solution manifest itself. The most comfortable path of exit from the morass in a practical direction was garbed in what might have been the cloak of *realism* or perhaps the "visionary" cover of the ideology of an altruistic mission. Zionism was bringing to the Orient

134

a Western culture, with its social attainments, its democratic methods of government, and its progressive economy. It could not be asserted that Zionism was displacing the Arabs. On the contrary, it was to bring them a blessing.

In this manner Zionism attempted to justify its penetration of Palestine and sweet-talk the opposition it aroused. This claim that an advantage was being provided to the Arabs by Zionism was much like that of assimilationist Jewry, which defended its right to existence among nations that rejected it by claiming a moral, religious mission on the part of Judaism. The fact that in Palestine the assertion of mission also had a certain reality did nothing to correct the fundamental delusion of the claim. This was a variation of the doctrine of a Jewish mission to the peoples of the world. It expressed that naive hope for harmony which existed only in the minds of the advocates of the doctrine.

These words are by no means to be interpreted as a denial of the Jewish people's moral right to Palestine. A nation does not have to apologize for aspiring to lead an independent existence. The Jewish people does not have to apologize for its ambition to rebuild its homeland in the land of Israel. This right, in and of itself, is understood by every Jew, and he has no need to justify himself before anyone in the world.

Nor was this a right lacking confirmation from outside the Jewish fold. People of European culture whose attitude toward the Jewish people was influenced by Christian tradition were able, to the same degree that they rejected the Jew in their own countries, to understand his cultural-historic right to Palestine. After the fact, they also extended political help

135

for the establishment of the Jewish State. The trouble
is that this right of the Jewish people clashed with the
rights of the Arab inhabitant. The Arab was never a
party to tangled Jewish-Christian relations. He was,
therefore, unable to understand it in a fundamental
way. Thus the rendering of justice to the Jewish people was bound up with a wrong for which Zionism is
not guilty in the full sense of the word. But the Zionist
movement is inevitably responsible for it.

A tragic situation was created, then, in which events
kept happening, adding one complication to another.
The Jewish pioneer, of course, had no idea of displacing the Arab inhabitant and felt no hostility toward
him from the start. He was prepared to live in peace
with his Arab neighbor. He also evidenced a goodwill
whose sincerity is not open to doubt. But as a rule he
tried to think about the Arab as little as possible. When
all was said and done, though, the presence of the
Jewish settler undermined the national right of the
Arab in Palestine. And that process of undermining
remained in force even when the Zionist movement
was very careful not only not to talk about it, but not
even to think about it.

On the other hand, the organized reaction of the
Arab community was one of hostility and ill will. The
Arab leadership refused to comprehend the Jewish
people's rights to Palestine and plotted violence
against Zionist settlement. On this basis, the Zionist
movement was correct when it repeatedly asserted
that the Arabs were the aggressors who took the initiative in every open struggle, while the Jews were pur-
suing peace. This was, nevertheless, a one-sided argument. It ignored the fact that Zionism had created the
condition which produced all these frictions. Zionism

had good cause to pursue peace while the Arabs—let us admit this—had cause to break the peace.

It must be reemphasized that the intention here is not to cast doubt on the justice of our actions in Palestine. We have been placed in a tragic situation in which right and wrong are tied together. And though we are ready for the wrong—because we feel we have no choice or because we give preference to the position of one whose righteousness consists in the fact that he is battling for his very survival—we will still be doing ourselves a favor if we admit our moral responsibility for the condition we have unintentionally created, and if we recognize how great a price we are paying and shall have to continue paying for it.

(But I should like to add that my views have changed since the Six-Day War. I can no longer accept this casting of the problem, as if a balance exists between the Arab and Jewish claims to Palestine. The consistent and grossly violent refusal of the Arabs to understand the Jews' problem and acknowledge their rights undermines the balance and places the entire issue in a new light. However, the tensely aggressive atmosphere that has been created by these relationships still exists in full force.)

From a situation of external tension between Jewish victims and Arab aggressors, we have passed to one between two sides ready to attack one another. This change has not brought normal relations between Israel and the nations of the world any closer. Of course, the situation of the Jew in Israel is not to be compared to his position in the Diaspora. In Israel he stands straight and feels strong and independent. But the decisive importance held by the army in the minds of Israel's citizens—and for them it is the expression of the main difference between homeland and Diaspora, as such taking on the air of a sacred value for many— clearly discloses the violence-laden tension under which we live. Our existence in this region is still not something to be taken for granted. The State of Israel is culturally alien to its environment. Its very existence is a thorn in the flesh of its neighbors. They look upon it as the embodiment of an act of injustice. Nor can this hostility be compared to the "normal" condition of enmity prevailing among other nations living side by side with one another for many generations, reconciled to the reality of their mutual proximity. Here we discern the denial of the very right of the Jewish State to exist where it does. Its environment treats it as an alien, precisely as European society, in an earlier period, treated the Jew who was trying to take his place as a citizen within it. In this situation we must keep up our strength against neighbors. And this fact increases our political dependence upon the support of nations outside our region. For it is only by their assistance that the threatening balance of power between the Arab states and ourselves may be maintained.

This fact has a far-reaching influence on our internal way of life as well. The extreme sense of mental preparedness, the continually mounting importance attributed to the security forces, and the anxiety for the assurance of survival which has in itself been made into a "value"—perhaps even a value before which many other values must give way—all these phenomena, the dangers of which keep on growing, derive their justification from the bitter antagonism which prevails between Israel and the other nations.

You might say that although there is no comparison

in all respects between our condition and that of the Jews of the Diaspora, we are no closer to normality here in Israel than we were outside it. We just face a new variation of an old question: Is there a way to remove the tension without depriving ourselves of the basic rights of the Jewish community in Palestine? Is it at all possible to diminish the dimensions of the wrong that has been done without endangering Israel's position, and thus bring about a rapprochement between Israel and her neighbors? Is there some way in which we can bridle the power of the security establishment—flowing as it does from the external hostility of the environment—over our public life? Can we prevent having all our social and intellectual activity turned into the direct function of a war of survival? These are penetrating questions. The answers to them will determine the fate of a Jewish community in regard to its political position as well as in respect to its inner condition.

(Today, after the Six-Day War, these questions have not only not disappeared, but have become all the more pressing.)

In a certain sense, the aspiration for normalization, of which Zionism is but one expression, attained success more fully in some of the Diaspora countries than anywhere else. In the Western democracies we see the gradual weakening of the feeling of foreignness as a result of the integration of the Jews into the economic, social, and cultural life of their surroundings. True, this process is still far from complete. After every step closer, there always remains a gap which most Jews cannot pass over in a single leap. The barrier which becomes more and more transparent and thin is nonetheless a barrier. Even what has so far been

139

accomplished is of doubtful quality. It cannot be considered as normalization in the sense in which Zionism—even the cultural centrists—employ the term. The process of approaching the environment's way of life involves assimilation. And that is already threatening the disintegration of large sections of the Jewish people.

At this point, then, the question arises from the other extreme. In the State of Israel, where there is no danger of Jewish loss of national identity, confinement within the frame of a separate cultural-political life has led to a situation of extreme antagonism with the environment. At the same time, in the Jewish communities of the Western democracies, the declining hostility of the environment has led to the demolishing of separate Jewish social structures. And it would seem that this is also difficult to define as a process of normalization when applied to a people that does not wish to forgo its survival.

The problem confronting the Jewish community abroad is how to establish a position of separateness without foreignness, of uniqueness without ghettoization. How can Jews preserve a full social framework for themselves, while at the same time achieving rapprochement and integration with their surroundings? One must admit that these are most difficult problems to solve. The preservation of a separate social structure is likely to make it more difficult for the Jew to become integrated into the economy and social life of his land of residence. The attempt at such preservation is therefore placed under the pressure of a very powerful force of attraction from outside. That force is almost irresistible. This sort of an ideological orientation, then, involves a great deal of artificial resistance to the "natural" processes taking place in the surroundings. It can achieve success only if the Jewish community in the Diaspora evidences a very great creative power. That power would have to be so strong that it would make the Jew capable of permanent existence under a certain measure of anomalous tension with his environment. For it is only anomaly which can make possible the continuation of Jewish life in the Galut.

(This problem, too, has lost none of its bite in the period following the Six-Day War. But it does seem to have been demonstrated that Israel can play a more active role in applying the brakes to the Diaspora's process of assimilation.)

Is Zionism capable of achieving that goal? A negative answer is inescapable when we judge the meaning of the spiritual center concept. Still, it is possible that the State, by its very existence, can provide encouragement and aid. However, the Diaspora would have to find its field of creativity within Israel in order to withstand the attractive power of the environment. The Galut would not, then, be made "normal" simply by virtue of the existence of a "normal" Jewish state in the land of Israel. Both here and there we are face to face with a reality that is far from normal, though in opposite directions. The problems that have arisen throw doubts not only on the unity but also on the very survival of the Jewish people.

The Normal Existence of the Jewish People
What conclusion, then, is to be drawn from the foregoing analysis? As has been said, there was a widespread feeling that Zionism's time was past because its role had been completely fulfilled or because the State of

Israel had taken over its functions to the point where it was left no field of activity. But a critique of this sort is not confirmed by our analysis. The tendency expressed in such a critique to place the State of Israel in the position of sole focus for Jewish life is mistaken and even fraught with peril. The logical conclusion from our analysis is just the opposite: Zionism did not completely fulfill the function it took upon itself, nor did the State inherit that function. The State merely fixed the limit of its capability.

The partial realization of the Zionist idea brings us into confrontation with that which cannot be realized. Most of the Jewish people continues to live in the Diaspora. The State of Israel is unable to serve as the spiritual center for all Jews. The polarity of choice between assimilation into the external environment and extreme self-segregation is still as strong as ever. The problem of the continuation of Judaism as a culture, or as an independent and unique religion, is not only unsolved but is even more severe than before.

We are dealing then with a historical chain of events, the flow of which cannot be fundamentally changed. The room that has been given the Jewish people among the nations of the earth (and the circumstances which created this condition are not within the scope of the present discussion) is sufficient to allow us to adjust by makeshift measures to each new political configuration. But it does not allow the Jewish people to integrate unobtrusively like one segment among all the others. It may be said that the goal of normalization of the life of the Jewish people, in keeping with the concepts of European nationalism, is ultimately unattainable. After rapprochement achieved its initial gains, it reached its limit. Then the tension of the Jew's feeling toward his environment, having dispersed somewhat during the course of his self-adjustment, became recharged.

(The possibilities revealed after the Six-Day War create an opportunity for the establishment of a different and more dynamic relationship between Israel and the Diaspora. Such a relationship could change the significance of the picture we have drawn. But we shall have more to say on this in the next chapter.)

Our statements are not to be taken as a protest against the tendency toward accommodation to modern political and cultural conditions. On the contrary, that tendency is vital. It even comprises a legitimate phenomenon in Jewish history. There is no period—including the Middle Ages, to which the philosophers of history are accustomed to point as an example of the segregation of Jewish society from its surroundings—in which there was no discernible aspiration for accommodating the organization of Jewish life to the concepts of the environment and its circumstances. But this tendency does not necessarily express a desire to ignore Jewish destiny and its unique significance as the history of the relationship between a chosen people and its God. Adjustment and accommodation do not imply assimilation or taking on the coloration of the environment. They do signify finding a way to assure the survival of the Jewish people and its freedom of creativity in any political context into which it might be propelled.

There is, then, no need to read off indictments against the Jew's aspiration to have his national organizations conform to the political structure of the modern age and to its cultural concepts. On the contrary, any attempt to demand that the Jew reconcile himself to a condition of insecurity or physical and intellectual discomfort not only has no chance of gaining the ear of the masses, but is also unethical. For this reason, Zionism was right in its diagnosis of the condition of European Jewry, whose very life was in danger of extinction and whose creative power was close to paralysis. Zionism was even right about the solution it proposed—because adjustment to the political structure of the modern age necessitated the establishment of an independent political center for the Jewish people. Without such a center there could be no guarantee of survival.

Zionism was not thinking only of adjustment, however. Its uniqueness as a revolutionary movement in Jewish history lies in its intention to have the Jewish nation *resemble* the rest of the segments which comprise the political system of modern times. And in this it was not successful. After the rapprochement that reached its peak with the establishment of the State, the swing back began. What had not been and could never be achieved now became apparent. The tension which had been relaxed through the effort of rebuilding the national home by postponing problems now became recharged, once it was plain that these problems were as real as ever.

This, then, is the full explanation of the ideological confusion which afflicted the Zionist movement after the creation of the State of Israel. Since such is the case, we have an obligation to bestir ourselves out of the rut of conditional arrangements and the routine of solutions, the whole force of which is in the direction of disregarding realities and providing excuses to postpone confrontations with problems because the problems are too hard, or because of our fear of the conclu-

144

sions that will have to drawn and applied practically. We must outline new methods of education and new lines of political and social action. And they must be based on the positive implications of Zionism and on the real needs of the State. But they must not be founded upon subordination or enslavement to the patterns of thought and action that have already been shaped within the State and the Zionist movement. As long as we show no willingness for this approach, we shall not find a way out of the morass.

7

A TIME OF RETURNING

*On the Religious Aspect of the Experience of
Triumph and Liberation*

Introduction

What happened to Israel in the time between the
celebration of the nineteenth anniversary of the Day
of Independence and the conclusion of the Six-Day
War? How easy, and yet how difficult, it is to answer
that question. It is easy to answer if our intent is
merely to point out the political and military events.
It is easy even if we aim at a description of the series
of events with all their dramatic twists—from a com-
placent sense of security that military confrontation
had nothing more to do with us, to the peril of immediate destruction, and from that to a military triumph the dimensions of which no one could have
guessed at the outset.

It is more difficult to respond to the question if the
intent is to grasp the full meaning of the change which
took place with the victory—from the political, national, and internal social points of view. The entire
pattern of relations between ourselves and the states
of our region was shaken, as was that with the great
powers and the various regional blocs. Much was altered also in the relations of Israel with Jewish com-

munities abroad. And the social and economic balance within the State of Israel changed more than a little.

But the process of crystallization of a new pattern of relationships has only just begun. It is still very much dependent on what will and will not be done in the near future. Therefore, anything that is said about it at this point is in the realm of theorizing or is the mere expression of what might be desirable.

It is hardest of all to describe or explain the quality of the experience we had during those short-long days. The whole people—every single individual of it, both those who fought at the front and those who remained in the rear—shared the awareness that they had experienced an extraordinary event—extraordinary in both its nature and its power. Something unexpected had occurred within, something mighty and marvelous; but what was that something? People who are accustomed to religious concepts, and do not feel hesitant about employing them, spoke of "a miracle." The more enthusiastic among them even spoke of the "start of the redemption" and the "messianic era," though it is not clear what they understood by those expressions, which have long been flowery clichés devoid of precise meaning.

But even people who do not regularly think in terms of religious concepts, or who feel hesitant about using such strange and unfamiliar words, gave testimony of an experience impinging on the religious. Of course, they tried to cover what seemed to them outlandish with a jocular tone or with embarrassed reserve, as though they were not permitted to employ terminology of that nature. Even so, they were forced into biblical language. "We were like unto them that dream . . ."—people who are not numbered among the reciters of psalms expressed themselves thus. And it appears that they were conscious of the significance of the context. There were even some who felt a need for a ritual gesture—a prayer or a thanksgiving ceremony. This demonstrates that their accustomed usages and observances would not do this time. They were compelled to delve into their cultural heritage, into strata which they had not taken possession of previously, except as mere areas of required knowledge which they had abandoned to the outer limits of forgotten school subjects, like beautiful but uninhabited places of antiquity.

A Spiritual Turning Point
with Continuity or a One-Time Event?

Would it not then be proper to describe this experience as a turning point? Did it not contain the potential for cultural reorientation and perhaps even for a public return to faith? Did it not, at the very least, offer some sort of break in the wall that separates the secularist from the religious community? And is not that change likely to wield a decisive influence on the shaping of our social and national life-style in the future?

It is certainly a naive error to assume (even if some people who are far from naive were caught up in that assumption during moments of enthusiasm) that words which are spoken in the heat of an experience can testify that a change has suddenly taken place in the spiritual orientation of the speaker. Such words cannot bear witness to one's readiness to reexamine one's way of life or views or judgments on matters of importance. A person's philosophy and manner of living cannot be changed overnight, not even under the influence of a great event. They express an entire complex of life experience, and such a complex cannot be radically altered in a single moment.

A great event can, therefore, shock a man and compel him to make a response that will surprise him. But when the tide ebbs, he becomes himself again. He returns to his regular habits and to his accustomed way of life. And then he also goes back to his former views. It is natural—and naive—to make the mistake of assuming that it is possible to transfer the one-time peak experience to day-to-day living. Such moments have no continuity in the simplistic sense of the concept. You cannot remain within them or perpetuate them. They happen at an hour when we have no control over their timing. And they are over before we know it. At the very moment when a man is stirred by the desire to stop time or to protract an experience in its pristine force, the descent to the everyday rut has already begun.

If a person stubbornly ignores this truth and remains on the peaks, he is then taken hold of by all the distortions of emotionalism and deceitful romanticism. Let us confess that we have not been free of such phenomena, nor shall we be in the near future. Furthermore, if the peak experience arises out of the routine life which a person leads, that experience cannot be totally alien to his life. The return to the previously accustomed paths of behavior and thought should therefore be quite easy and uncomplicated. Those remote cultural strata which came near us for a brief moment should once again be relegated to some distant corner, and the world should get back to normal.

On the basis of our own experience, we can already debate at present to what extent this statement may be correct. Of course, we are far from the old routine.

We are still refusing to wake up from the dream, nor are we even *able* to awaken from it. No new routine has yet crystallized—in the political, national, or social areas—to take the place of the former fashions which have, in large measure, been swept away. We have still not attained a waking reality, as distinguished from the reality of the dream. But even in this condition of twilight sleep, a condition somewhere between unexpected awakening and fading dreaminess, the vast majority of the population has already sobered up on matters having to do with its philosophy of life.

Styles of cultural evaluation have not changed. The causes of tension between religionists and secularists remain as they were. And the ambivalent evaluation, of national values on the one side and religious values on the other, has not been altered either.

Reflection as a Way
of Carrying On the Experience

Nonetheless, we ought to be wary of hyperbolized sobriety, that which can cause a person to prefer the prose of daily living to the poetry of momentary experience. Even if such moments cannot be protracted in a straightforward manner, there *is* a way to use them to extend and enrich everyday life without emotionalism or romanticism. Moreover, through that method their influence is even deepened and their importance magnified.

And what is that way? By reflection. This is a reexperiencing of the event by summoning it to the imagination and thought. Reflection on the past, of course, has no power to reactualize the original experience. But in a certain sense it offers more than the experience itself did. This is because consciousness customarily lags behind sensation. One's consciousness

151

reflects back on the object at a distance and delves into its meaning. Only after leisurely consideration and examination can one effectuate a change in his personal philosophy and patterns of behavior. Furthermore, just as it is impossible to perpetuate the experience, so is it impossible to erase completely the impression it leaves.

The return to everyday life is never a mere going back to the previous situation. Something has been added to the totality of the person's experience. Potentialities, the reality of which he had not previously guessed at, are revealed to him. And perhaps there is also created in him a doorway to conditions, emotions, and beliefs which had earlier been alien or completely incomprehensible to him. Those layers of cultural heritage which had come so close for an hour have, of course, again been relegated to an obscure corner. But they will never again be just a theoretical school subject; they can never go back to being "uninhabited places." Traces of life have now appeared in them. They have now shown themselves worthy of human habitation. This opening is, of course, not an achievement of a firm and stable nature. It certainly contains nothing to assure such an achievement—but it does offer an opportunity. It is possible progressively to erect a structure of philosophy and action on it—though, of course, the actualization or neglect of this chance is a matter of free decision.

If it is our desire, then, to hold on to the inner happening which has been ours—to rescue it from oblivion and turn it into a keystone of our life structure—we must go back and reflect on it. We must go back and explore what happened to us during those days. Why did we respond as we did? What potentialities

152

showed themselves in us, and how can we make them a reality in our lives?

The War of Independence and the Six-Day War

In describing the uniqueness of a fundamental experience and analyzing its meanings, we require comparisons with similar experiences which preceded it and form its background. If the truth be told, such a comparison is made simultaneously with the sensation itself. Even during it we already sense, if only in a dull fashion, the special nature of the moment in contrast to what went before. Even if we do not yet place the details of one event over against those of the other, we are aware of parallels and differences. We arrange impression opposite impression. Later consideration continues the sensation in its own way in this sense also: it clarifies and highlights that reflective impetus which the experience contained from the start, and it makes real the perspective which is in the sensation itself.

To what event can we compare the Six-Day War? For a large part of the Israeli public—that part which was born in Israel or which immigrated before the establishment of the State or immediately thereafter —the War of Independence is the event of which one naturally thinks. The Six-Day War is experienced with a consciousness of the ways it is similar or dissimilar to the War of Independence. The inner perspective of that experience stretches between those two wars. It is, therefore, only right that later reflection begins with a comparison of them.

153

Like and Unlike

What are the similarities between the two wars, or in what ways was the second war a continuation of the first? In both wars the Jewish community of the land of Israel fought for its very existence and for preservation of its political achievements. In both wars Israel fought against the Arab states and other hostile international elements which supported the Arab states for more or less similar motives. In both wars a political fact was created which had far-reaching and revolutionary results from the national and international points of view. In both wars we exhausted the full capacity that was in us, and the feeling of identification of the various segments of the Jewish people reached its peak. Beyond all this, the Six-Day War was caused by political facts that had been determined by the War of Independence. In some aspects, the later war may be viewed as a second stage of the earlier one, a stage in which the partial attainments of the War of Independence were brought to completion. These lines of resemblance and connection justify the drawing of parallels. But those parallels only serve to point up the differences which make the recent war unique.

Let us start with an external point which immediately strikes one: the difference in duration. The War of Independence was a relatively short conflict—but compared to the Six-Day War it was quite long. This difference goes far in determining the degree of intensity and the balance among the various conflicting elements that make up war and victory.

The War of Independence was a comparatively slow occurrence. Each phase took place separately. And even though the general context was one of tri-

154

umph, the retreats and defeats in battle were very sharply realized. Final victory in the War of Independence was therefore achieved with great difficulty, and that difficulty considerably dampened the joy of achievement.

That was not true of the Six-Day War. There the final result was attained with almost a single sweep. The partial failures, if such happened here and there, were swallowed up in the total unconditional success. Even our pain over those who fell could not penetrate our consciousness during the course of the fighting. The mourning came after victory was complete and total. So our grief took on the dimension of a profound chasm on a mountaintop. We experienced everything at once in a state of shock in which laughter and tears mingled. The speed of events made the nature of the historical turning point even more dramatic. The new situation was created so suddenly and was so completely different in all respects from what had just preceded it. Therefore, we experienced with extreme intensity the very radical nature of change brought about by the event. It was as if we had skipped over a whole process that had only just been started and found ourselves on the other side of a fortified wall. That fact had its effect on the character and coloration of the sensation we felt during the Six-Day War. It had a deep effect.

From Height to Valley
and Back Again

We have said that the War of Independence was of relatively short duration, but we did not give a precise judgment. The War of Independence was not an isolated happening but the last link in a long chain of events. Battle followed battle. And even during periods of relative quiet our immense efforts were unceasing—the effort for settlement, the upbuilding of the land, the increase of immigration, and the political struggle with the mandatary power. Each step demanded great personal sacrifices. And the successes were accompanied by failures and retreats, internal self-criticism and tense preparation. The War of Independence, which crowned the years of effort with victory, demanded all our strength. And it must not be forgotten that there were many refugees of the Holocaust among us who had come to Palestine shortly before the establishment of the State. For them, this was literally their last strength. Clearly, this fact brought predictable results, both during the war and after it. Everyone responded according to his capacity. The native-born young people, for whom this was the first big test, answered with very great devotion.

But the burden was heavy. When the battles were over, weariness was everywhere—especially among the young people upon whose shoulders the weight of the front-line fighting had fallen. This does not imply that they would have been unable to continue fighting if that had been required of them. However, they were no longer needed for war but for the building of the State. This demanded a spiritual willingness of another sort—which was apparently not in them. They, too, were swept along with the rest on a wave of frustration, bitterness, and guilt feelings.

Be that as it may, the victory awakened a demand for personal compensation in the heart of every individual. Everyone sought to see the material results of the triumph for himself, not just in terms of gain for the society but also in terms of personal profit. The unbridled race for higher living standards and the acquisition of social status gave active expression to this desire. The fact that the political achievement was too small to provide the demands that everybody was making on everybody else, and the fact that the universal struggle for the fulfillment of those demands was endangering the very existence of what had been achieved did not serve as restraining factors. On the contrary, bitter feelings and frustrations increased, the competition among both organized groups and individuals grew, and to the personal insatiable hunger, guilt feelings and self-hatred were added. In his own mind, each person felt that he was right only in relation to the other fellows, who were behaving just as he was. In essence he knew that his behavior was petty and degraded.

Such, it seems, is the background for the sprouting of the myth that was with us for the State of Israel's first nineteen years. That fairy tale taught that until the War of Independence the Jewish community in Palestine was a collection of sublime human beings; our life was one of spiritual fulfillment, saturated with the tension of preparedness for great ideals and fraught with awareness of personal self-worth—but after the War of Independence it all collapsed from within. We became (so runs the story) pursuers of honors and power, scurrying after status and high living, mired in the mud of treachery and double-dealing, devoid of spiritual life and a sense of self-esteem.

Such a distinction between one period and the next is no doubt an oversimplification. But even if it is nothing more than a myth, it still faithfully reflects many people's sense of reality after the creation of the State. No one dared to say the unutterable openly, but the accomplishment seemed smaller than had been an-

157

ticipated. It did not have equal weight on the emotional scales with the effort that had been invested in it. Was this the realization of the great dream of Zionism—a country cruelly and unnaturally dismembered? A state bounded by twisted borders and choked by hostility? A land unable to solve from the start, even in part, the problems of Jewry and Judaism which Zionism had boasted of solving? A state so tiny that it was unable to offer even the personal compensation due those who were ready to give their lives for it?

If we had seen things in the proper light, we would have said that this was not the achievement itself but only the painful beginning, and that one must add sacrifice in the effort to build, settle, and absorb, so as to bring it to completion. But at that time there did not appear to be any chance of attaining peace and stability, and thus open the door for completion of the goal. Nor was there any inner readiness to continue making personal sacrifices. Therefore, we lived with the achievement as if it were complete, and we demanded of it what we would have had a right to demand without self-degradation only from the truly finished work.

Such was not the case in the Six-Day War. It broke out after nineteen years of relaxation of tension and found us weary of stupid routine and of a decline which had, in its last stages, put on the garb of disintegration. And then, with a shake of the head, the old Yishuv got back its original drive. Its children again became what they had envisioned themselves as being. Once more, a generation grew great in its own eyes—in its willingness for self-sacrifice and devotion. It had never guessed at the presence of those qualities within itself because they had never been put to the practical test.

Accomplishment
Greater than Anticipation

What did we hope for in that war—consciously? For the preservation of the status quo, nothing more. But on this occasion, not just the expected was realized. This time the great things for which we no longer hoped became realities. The program drawn up in Zionism's original vision—return to the ancestral land in order to rebuild the nation—suddenly became a tangible possibility and a direct challenge. For the whole country was in our hands, in full magnitude, in its total historic presence. It was now possible to effectuate the solution which Zionism had proposed from the start.

It was for that reason "we were like unto them that dream." For certainly one who sees with his own eyes the materialization of an ambition for which he no longer even dared hope must be dreaming. Was not this what we desired? We now say that it was surely what we desired. We wanted it all along. But just a few weeks earlier we did not dare want what we desired. We did not dare set ourselves a goal which seemed to us to be beyond the boundaries of the possible. This time, therefore, the achievement was greater than that which had been anticipated. It outweighed sevenfold the effort that had been invested. And if the earlier partial achievement, which came after the application of all our powers, had led to a fading of preparedness for the future and to a scorning of potential disaster because of an aim to exploit the present, the total achievement, which did not exhaust our powers, now came and once more mustered the old spirit of willingness. Now, once again, we stand called by duty before a future to which the present is a threshold. It is within our power to will a total desire and to choose what we want to be.

Israel and the Diaspora

During the period of upbuilding before the creation of the State, Palestine was a focus of world Jewish activity. This was so because the Jewish community in Palestine directly represented the Diaspora. The continuation of the upbuilding of the land was dependent on the continued Zionist education and on the organizational, social, political, and economic action of the Zionist movement abroad. During that period, therefore, Palestine came to serve as a spiritual, political, and social center for at least that segment of the Jewish people which joined together out of consciousness about Zionism. With the establishment of the State, at the moment when the hope of turning Palestine into the spiritual center of the Jewish people had apparently taken shape, a drastic change also occurred in this respect. For all practical purposes, Palestine ceased serving as a focus for overall Jewish activity.

External processes brought about this phenomenon. There was, for example, acclimatization of Jews in the Western Hemisphere and Europe, as well as the raising of an iron curtain around the Jews of the Soviet Union. But the political, social, and cultural atmosphere of Israel also had more than a little bearing on the issue. The Israeli community no longer represented the Diaspora directly, and the Yishuv's existence no longer depended directly on the continuation of Zionist education or continued organized activity on the part of the Zionist movement overseas. In fact, a separate political framework was created, eliciting the demand for cessation of "outside" intervention. It is also true that life in Israel lost its radiant force because of the downtrend in social and spiritual life which we discussed previously. Israel therefore became, even for the Jewish people, a sort of province, interest in which progressively waned.

But the Six-Day War also brought about a change in this regard. The Jewish Diaspora revealed anew how vital, in respect to its Jewish identification, it considered the existence of the State of Israel to be. At the same time, the State itself was summoned again to old-new challenges. Now the State of Israel once more can serve as a spiritual center and a focus of world Jewish activity.

The Adherence of Native Israelis
to Jewish Tradition

It must be said that from an all-inclusive historical viewpoint the War of Independence was the end of an era, after which there was a decline. But the Six-Day War was the beginning of an era, which carries with it the opportunity for ascendancy. However, from the standpoint of the young generation that was born in the land, and also perhaps from the standpoint of those who participated actively in the War of Independence, that war was the beginning of an era, while the Six-Day War marked a midpoint—a midpoint from which a reevaluation of both the past and the future is possible.

The generation which reached its early years of maturity during the War of Independence was educated almost in its entirety on the bedrock of the ideology of Labor Zionism. This education imparted to them knowledge and rational conviction about the correctness of that ideology, and it implanted a general awareness of belonging to the Jewish people and to Jewish culture. But rational conviction and vague national consciousness did not provide a total determinant—emotional or intellectual—within either the Zionist movement or Jewish culture. The direct personal experience which does provide such a determinant was not within its grasp.

That generation was not tested in the reality of the Galut, from which the roots of the Zionist experience drew sustenance. It never led a life of discomfort of the kind on which socialist doctrine is based. Nor was that generation grounded in that Jewish tradition which can foster an exalted sense of identification with the Jewish people.

In what way, then, *was* that generation tested? By the immediate danger that lay in wait for the Yishuv from both the Arabs and the mandatary power. That was its experience and that was what determined the fact of its participation in *war* as a thing taken for granted. About that, there was no room for argument. But from this fact the sensation of belonging to the nation was drawn. Identification with the overall national objectives did not follow from this experience. On the contrary, it was the personal trial in battle which demonstrated to the young native-born Jew how different he was from his parents in respect to Zionism, the Jewish people, and Jewish culture. He was unable to see the accomplishment of his own personal desires in the achievement of the objectives of Zionism. His own aims were different. And even if he could not always formulate them clearly (in large measure because he had been educated in a certain ideology and his language did not suit his inner experience), it was plain that they were all included in the category of personal fulfillment in the life of the present and in private life, not in the category of expectations for the national future. In the view of the vast majority of that generation, Zionism was, therefore, a just cause in its own right. But it was a cause that did not directly and personally touch them. For them, it was a matter of secondary importance.

It is obvious that their response to the establishment of the State of Israel and to its rescue from enemy hands was not the "messianic" reaction of their parents. That age group did not feel that this was "a Jewish state after two thousand years of exile." Two thousand years of Galut did not involve them. And the prophetic pathos with which their parents responded to the event seemed garish and inflated to them even during the fighting, and even more so afterwards. Nor did the mere act of being alive in the State cause elation, because this fact had no direct significance for the way of life of the individual.

At this point we come upon the basic explanation for the fact that the overwhelming majority of the younger generation did not find their place in life within those limits where pioneering activity was still required. This is also the basic reason why the ambition for personal goals, strong as it may have been, was accompanied by feelings of frustration, emptiness, and guilt. As long as the fighting was going on, the young people could dissociate themselves from their parents' way of life, and they could revolt against the ideals by which they had been educated—all without losing their sense of self-respect. This was possible for that age group because the acts they were performing at the time were still tied to the old ideals. By those acts they earned the right to criticize.

163

But after the war there was nothing against which one could even meaningfully rebel. Nor was there any ideal to take the place of those by which they had been brought up. On the contrary, they well knew that Israel needed not only people who would be ready to die for it but those who were prepared to live in and for it. Many of the parents—but only a few of the children—were thus prepared. And one who recognizes his obligation, and at the same time knows that he cannot respond to it without compelling himself to take a path that is alien to his own spirit, will lead a life marked by guilt, emptiness, and failure. The literature of this generation testifies to this fact clearly and almost unanimously.

Reawakening of the Consciousness of Belonging to the Nation and Its Heritage

It is difficult to determine with certainty, but it seems that there was also a different spirit in the Six-Day War in respect to a reawakening of the consciousness of belonging to the nation and its heritage. A dimension of historical identification showed itself which was in no sense present during the War of Independence. The worn-out phrase "a Jewish state after two thousand years of exile" was no longer a cliché. And the rest of the concepts that had been stripped of significance also became recharged with meaning. Now it not only mattered that the Jewish community would continue to exist; but it was also important that the Jewish State survived, that the whole land of Israel had been liberated, and that a reunified Jerusalem—as a national historical symbol—should be its capital. It is still too early to tell whether that sense of concern will have an effect on the daily life of the private citizen.

Be that as it may, there is weight to the fact that our acts demonstrated a historical perspective, and that in this respect a partnership of shared experience was created between traditionally educated Jews who had returned from the Galut and native sons not thus educated.

What brought about this change? Maturity, of course, played a part. A young person with little experience and few memories cannot compare with a mature man with much experience and rich memories. The latter knows well the significance of the dimension of the past. Nor can resistance to the danger of extermination at an age at which a person is not even responsible for himself compare to the same experience when one bears the responsibilities for one's children, family, and entire community. Associations with time and societal ties by which the mature man lives have become broader and more inclusive. He does not, therefore, react as does a child or youth on the basis of his own limited "I" which may demand immediate satisfaction. His ego is broader. Past and society and culture are reflected in it. They shape its desires and objectives. From this point of view, the literature of the veterans of the War of Independence was that of youngsters who refuse to grow up. In the Six-Day War that generation reached its period of spiritual maturity.

But we do not seem to have exhausted the subject with these remarks. There is a further difference on which rests the foundation of all the differences which we previously pointed out between the two wars. The War of Independence marked the start of a process of estrangement and alienation of the Israeli community —and perhaps of Jews abroad as well—from their own point of origin. Individuals were estranged from their own fundamental experience, and the community from its historic destiny. In the course of the nineteen years of the existence of the State, the process of alienation had reached a peak. But in the meantime something had happened in the life of individuals and in that of the community. There had been both an inner fermentation and emotional and intellectual struggling. Though these might not have been obvious in their full dimensions, they still left their imprint on us. And then came the Six-Day War and awakened us in a single stroke from the oblivious slumber that had been so disgustingly easy. The war forced us out of our depression and brought us back to the starting point. We went back to being what we had been—but we were nevertheless very different.

Return to the Point of Origin
Return to the point of origin—what does it mean? We must examine profoundly this word return, which has many, many connotations in Hebrew.

First of all, we experienced a return of that instinct which causes one to fight for survival itself. When we once again reflect on the period between the two wars, it becomes clear to us that the awareness of our need to fight for survival itself in the face of a hostile environment—one which was not prepared to reconcile itself with our presence in its midst—had been with us all the while. This had not, of course, taken the form of fear. The individual Jew no longer encountered enmity from the Arab population on a daily direct basis, as he did in the period of the British Mandate. And the responsibility for security was placed on government, not imposed on each citizen from day to day. It was therefore possible to get one's mind off the danger.

But what was put out of mind remained known and accompanied one like a shadow, especially since it was being intentionally and consciously ignored. Being aware of this, we can explain the special emotional relationship of the Israelis to their army. There was an attitude common to all elements in the population, including the intellectual element. An army is nothing more than a mechanism. It is an asset, not a value. But even those who understood this, even if they stressed it night and day, looked upon the Israel Defense Army, more than any other government agency, as a symbol of Jewish sovereignty. And being a symbol has a way of adding a sense of value to an asset. From time to time this attitude manifested itself in practice. This happened not only at the annual Independence Day parades, which were central to the celebration of the event, but at every mobilization. The response to the call-up for the Sinai campaign testified to this attitude in an especially prominent manner. But even responses to regular call-ups for service in the reserves revealed a clear inner relationship. People who showed cynicism toward the State in their routine lives and people who outwardly recognized no moral obligation to remain citizens of the country—they were ready for emigration without hesitation—willingly answered when they were summoned for service in the army. Anyone who recognized these signs could not have been surprised by the overall response to the mobilization order in the last war; there was something about it almost like the joy of fulfilling a mitzvah.

It seems, then, that the war experience, as a memory of the recent past and a permanent source of opportunity, has been with us all along. It was the fundamental sensation of the Israeli Jewish community. (Incidentally, Israeli literature never freed itself of war as a dominant theme which it examined and reexamined directly and indirectly again and again.) What is more, every reaction to the danger of immediate war always revealed a complete readiness that was the diametric contradiction to the perverse practices of daily life. The time of war was, therefore, "the moment of truth."

This conflict between evasion of duty in everyday life and total response in times of peril may seem odd to the casual observer. But for one who reflects deeply and sees things from the inside it is not at all surprising. The source of this phenomenon lies in the condition of one who is placed in continual danger of extermination for a long period of time. A person's first response to the threat of extermination is fear, and that response remains in full force as long as the danger remains latent and is not carried out in practice. Under such circumstances a person recoils and searches for a path of escape. Among the causes of the moral decline which occurred throughout the first nineteen years of the State's existence was the weariness with the struggle and fighting which failed to bring about a stable and secure peace. The battle was not decisively concluded. Beyond the relative tranquility lay the danger that we might be forced to fight for our existence a second and a third time. Complacency and shirking were, therefore, consciously or unconsciously, kinds of searches for shelter from peril. Inner degeneracy and outward emigration were unadorned escape in the literal sense of the word.

168

But fear is an initial reaction to a danger which is not immediate. When that danger materializes, fear is likely to be replaced by an opposite reaction. When a man has no way out of a battle in which he must defend his very life—and if he believes in his ability to win, even though the price be great—all his powers are brought to their height. At such a moment, fear may give way to courage. A feeling of fulfillment may replace flight from duty. And that feeling flows from the decisive assurance a man gains when he knows that he is carrying out what he really must do. It seems that when one is up against mortal danger from which one cannot save himself by flight, he senses a total awareness of his own being. His entry into battle is then an act of realization of the freedom to choose life. It is a time in which the person's entire life focuses into a single point of the present. It is, therefore, a moment when a man sometimes even feels the paradoxical emotion of terrifying self-fulfillment.

Return to the Point of Composition
Secular Zionism's Estrangement
From Jewish Tradition

Before we turn to the meaning of these experiences, we must again delve into our reflections on the sensation of return to the point of origin in respect to another condition which grew up between the wars. So far we have spoken of a return to a point of historical-biographical origin by the Jewish community in Israel. However, it appears that the Six-Day War brought about a transition in this area also. It is possible that the war activated a latent hope of returning to a more distant point of origin, one beyond the limited history of the Yishuv and outside the personal biographies of most of its individuals. Until now this point of origin has been borne in the memory inherited by each generation from its forebears. That is, it has come down through the information each individual received from study and reading alone in the cultural and historical heritage of the Jewish people. Indeed, the tragic discontinuance of this tradition is the prime cause of most of the inner processes that have affected the Jewish people in modern times. A great many of the people who came to Palestine before the establishment of the State were brought up in the tradition and then cut off from it, though they tried to continue it in their own way. The deeper they took root in the life of the country, the more they strayed from that tradition and the more they became alienated from it— even though, in a certain sense, they viewed their work as if it were a continuation of Jewish tradition.

The group which grew up and had its education in Palestine was distant from the tradition from the start. Its members never lived it. They learned about it— and little enough even of that. Perhaps they acquired a sense of the pain of its loss from their parents, whether this came to them consciously or merely as a sensation. Be that as it may, the sense of alienation from the traditional Jewish heritage increased during the first nineteen years of the existence of the State of Israel. It was as if the Jewish community in the land of Israel was a new departure that had no roots in what had gone before. But the wall of estrangement seemed to break down during the war. Individuals sensed their attachment to the past, beyond the point at which it had broken off.

Grasping Israel's Unique Fate

One of the aspects of return in the sense in which we have been using the word is the recognition, on the basis of direct personal experience, of the unique destiny of the Jewish people among the nations. A modern Jew who has been educated in European culture has great difficulty in accepting the traditional concept of the distinctiveness of the Jewish people as a divinely chosen people. It is difficult for him both because he is not prepared to reconcile himself with the fate that is implied in this distinguished position and because the concept does not fit into his philosophical system, be it socialist or liberal-humanist. It is all the harder because the upbuilding of the Jewish community in the land of Israel (like the building of the Jewish community in America and the rebuilding of the Jewish community in Europe after two world wars) has been carried out in a setting of aspiration for the normalization of the life of the Jewish people.

The rift between the modern Jew and the heritage of his fathers has truly focused on this point. This is a rift that has widened in proportion to the success with which the ambition for normalization has taken tangible form in Israel as well as in the United States and Europe. The Jewish people has apparently approached the condition of a "normal people" in several senses of the term, integrating itself into its environment and not segregating itself within its own destiny. Although the European Holocaust testified otherwise, that event brought about a growth in the aspiration for total normalization and provided indisputable justification for that concept. It was manifestly impossible to make peace with a distinctive role if this was its result. The years following the Holocaust opened doorways in every direction to the delusion that the desire for normalization had indeed been realized in great measure and that a holocaust for Jews was no longer possible in this world.

The Six-Day War came as a frightening shock for those who had been wrong on this point. First, the naive assumption that a holocaust was inconceivable was destroyed. The terrifyingly slow weeks, during which we anxiously waited for a decision to be made, indelibly engraved this fact upon the consciousness of every member of the nation.

Once again we found ourselves alone in the world. Part of that world—the active part—was hostile. Part of it was sympathetic, but that part withheld a helping hand which could be securely grasped. And part was "neutral," that is, indifferent. Our very existence was placed in danger, and we had nothing on which to depend except our own strength. So were we, then, a nation "like all the nations?" Had our historic fate changed at all?

There was another side, a very clear one, to this drama. Suddenly there stood up a little state of three million people, a country of Jews; and, because of its Jewishness, it found itself in the middle of an international thicket, standing on stage with everyone watching. Every act or omission of that state held significance for the whole world. In the land of Israel, where we had expected to achieve normalization, we were propelled (and not for the first time) into the crossroads of international interests. We were forced into the role of focal point in a cultural and religious clash. And the fact of our Jewishness isolated us in a hostile world.

At that moment our consciousness was apologetically withdrawing from its earlier certainties. And it was hard to keep from drawing the astonishing, amazing historical analogy: here we are, living in a time which reflects thousands of years of Jewish history.

Was Zionism, then, in principle a movement that led in the direction of normalization? According to its announced aim, yes. But, if so, why did it so persistently push itself into no other place than Palestine. Why into that focus of tension among nations and religions? Should not the outcome of such intransigence have been apparent from the beginning? Was this not caused by the desire to preserve the distinctive character of the Jewish people—in spite of everything? It must be said that Zionism, in regard to its relationship to the Jewish heritage, did not lead to normalization in the simplistic sense in which the word may be used of other peoples, but in the more complex, problematic sense in which it can be applied to the inner law which distinguishes Jewish history from that of the nations of the world.

Zionism therefore caused, without intending to do so, a reformulation of the same tense condition. During the weeks that passed between the start of the crisis and the beginning of the political struggle following our victory, it was hard to get this idea out of one's mind. This was the case even though the idea stood in extreme contradiction to our regular thought patterns. Our immediate experience rose up in rebellion against the viewpoint which we had attempted to force upon it.

The Memory of the Holocaust

But an additional factor inserts itself at this point, bearing witness to something that had become entrenched in our emotional and intellectual memories throughout the nineteen years of the existence of the State. The Six-Day War brought home to us the unity of destiny of the Jewish people in all generations by way of the prism of memory of the Holocaust. We had

173

been fleeing from that memory for years, and yet it pressed itself across the threshold of our consciousness. And we do not speak only of those who lived through the Holocaust with their own bodies. The educational effect of learning by study alone is perhaps not very strong. The impression it leaves in the mind is soft and weak. But the power of a serious crisis to set even a weak impression and imprint it in the consciousness as if it had been a direct experience is great. Education has great strength if it can help a person understand the full meaning of a crisis which is taking place before his very eyes. Such a crisis occurred during those weeks of waiting. And the memory of the Holocaust forced upon Israelis an understanding of the full meaning of what was happening. Knowledge of the Holocaust was thus set like a direct inner experience, even upon the minds of people who had not lived through it personally. It was that which imparted a nearly apocalyptic depth to the sense of crisis.

Identity with
the Destiny of the People

Thus we lived the Six-Day War through the prism of memory of the Holocaust. But in a way it was different from that memory. The decisive difference thrust itself out of the analogy. This time we stood with weapons in our hands. And despite the threat, it was plain that there was to be no Holocaust. The supernormal peculiarity of the Jewish fate?—without doubt. But this time the scales of miraculous history were moving to the opposite pole, from the depths of incredible tragedy to the heights of incomparable triumph. In the case of the Holocaust, even the believer could uncover no religious significance, much less give a

174

theological justification of divine justice. In the case of the triumph, on the other hand, even an unbeliever was likely to discover a higher significance above the profane political meaning of events—and to accept such a higher explanation even if it contradicted his former thought patterns.

After the event it is easy to point at a victory and say: "Behold, the historic uniqueness of a chosen people has been demonstrated." But was there a readiness among us before the event to give recognition to this uniqueness and to identify with it? Today we can look back and say that there was a bit of preparation for all this and that the entirety of that preparation was an impression left by very general and problematic study. (We shall return to this subject.) But total willingness and practical identification certainly did not exist. If the war had ended in defeat, or in a partial victory like the War of Independence, our opposition to the idea of the uniqueness of the Jewish people would certainly have flared up again hotter than ever. Now that history has responded to us so generously and our uniqueness has been embodied in such a marvelous victory—one that seems almost like a miracle to us—we find it possible to reconcile ourselves to the concept of a chosen people and to say yes from the bottom of our warm hearts.

A Change in the Evaluation
of Tradition

Along with the awareness of the distinctive nature of the destiny of the people of Israel, a second change occurred. In this factor, too, one can see an outgrowth of the deposit of emotional and intellectual memories that were saved up all through the first nineteen years

175

of Israel's existence. At the beginning of this chapter, we spoke of the intentional cutting loose from the Jewish heritage and of the revolt against it on the part of secular Zionism. But certain processes in the society and culture caused a reorientation in this regard with the establishment of the State. First of all, the bitterness of the criticism of Galut life flagged on the part of that generation which had revolted against it and had come to settle in Palestine. Maturity did a great deal to bring this about, and so did the destruction of the Jewish communities of the Galut. A nostalgia for the past soon showed itself and took on strength because of the feeling of frustration with the present, devoid of interest and hope for the future as it seemed to be. Both public and private life wallowed in matters of the present. So it was only natural for an examination to begin on what might shape life and give it meaning. One asked whether because of radical criticism something important had been neglected. Were there, perhaps, values without which an independent culture could not exist, without which one could never have a culture that would satisfy man's desire for a full private and public life?

This question was being asked not only by parents who reflected on what they had received from their own parents and what they were bequeathing their children, but also by the children themselves. The children had begun to be aware of the growing distress caused by the vacuum that was around them. Had not their parents kept back from them the basic cargo that had been carried along on the Zionist path? Had not the fathers and mothers withheld from their sons and daughters that attachment to Jewish content without which a full life could not be constructed in the here and now? Furthermore, the question of the Jewish identity of the State of Israel and its inhabitants was brought up with excessive gravity. Along with it came the problem of the cultural unity of the segment of the Jewish people inside Israel with that portion which remained outside.

These questions were subjected to widespread public discussion during the first nineteen years of Israel's existence. Their investigation gave rise to several experiments to readjust the contents of Jewish tradition to the modern life of a community which was not religious in the Orthodox sense of the word.

Perhaps the best known of these experiments was the attempt to insert and define the *Toda'a Yehudit* (Jewish consciousness curriculum) in the public school system. But this was not the most important experiment. Attempts at organizing various circles that were quite removed from one another were much more important. These circles discussed Jewish identification, deepened their Jewish knowledge through individual or guided study, and searched for ways to impart some traditional coloration to the Sabbath and festivals, as well as to important occasions in public and private life. Such experiments increased in recent years. This came with the intensification of political stress between the religious and the secular parties. Hand in hand with the opposition to moves to compel the adoption of Jewish religious law in the legislation of civil law, the desire to fit values from the tradition into daily life grew stronger and stronger.

The Ambiguity of
the Change—and Its Worth

We shall surely miss the truth if we fail to point out the soft and ambiguous character of this process. Can we say that it was in the nature of a penitent return? Yes and no. Yes, because the search expressed a true need. After the fact, it brought about the partial adoption of values which had been vigorously—and sometimes even snceringly—thrust aside. No, because the emotional and intellectual causes of the gap between the modern Jew and his ancestral culture had not disappeared in the least, nor had their operation ceased. It was patently impossible to cancel out people's attachment to humanistic cultural values or socialist principles. These systems had been given a position—because of the historic development of the Jewish people in modern times—in an area opposed to tradition. Or at least it was opposed to the philosophy of life of the carriers and shapers of the tradition during this period. A secular Jew who had been educated in European culture was, therefore, most likely to sense the chasm between himself and the tradition of his fathers precisely at the moment when he was trying to accommodate himself again to that tradition. What he could least of all accept in the traditional doctrine was its all-encompassing, total, obligatory nature—but only after such acceptance could the tradition's development and revival be carried on from within.

For these reasons, the experiments described here remained quite partial and problematic. They were far from solving the problem of the tragic gap between the Jewish people and its past. But though they were tentative, they created something in the minds of many: the inner background for an intense experience that was to surprise even those who underwent it. On the basis of these hesitant experiments, many who called themselves secularists were able to recognize the religious grounding of their own nationalistic sensations. And they were able to give expression to those sensations in terms of traditional symbols. The profound vibration that was felt, by people who were quite far from tradition, at the time of the liberation of the Temple Mount could not have happened without this background. Even though the sensation came as a shock to the very people who received it, they were clearly aware of the connection. In this regard it seems that what counted was not the intensiveness of the return to tradition—that remained superficial— nor its compass—that remained partial—but its positive direction. What had its effect was the mere act of opening the heart. That is what led to the stammered outburst at the Western Wall: "I am not religious. . . . I was never religious . . . but. . . ." The deposit of difficulties stored up throughout the first nineteen years of the existence of the State of Israel was summed up in that "but."

The Religious Significance
of the Experience of War
and Victory
At the Threshold of Faith

Let us now return to a consideration of the significance of the experience of war and victory. First, let it be borne in mind that taking a stand in a war of survival puts one on the threshold of faith. The imminent peril of death divests a person of the delusion which accompanies him throughout the normal routine of daily living. He may have deluded himself with the thought that his existence was automatically secure and permanent and that he had the natural right, inplicit in his very consciousness, to choose what is desirable and reject whatever is strange or painful.

179

But survival suddenly appears as a delicate, transparent tissue suspended in empty space. Any shock may destroy it, the least sudden blow can smash it. From whence did existence come? From a mysterious region of which we have no knowledge and over which we have no control. And what can guarantee its continuation? Not a thing! The person suddenly realizes that he has been *placed* in this world. Placed, in the sense that he is a being without his own consent according to an unknown will. And he can be removed from this world at any moment in keeping with that unknown will, or in accord with blind chance. At any moment. He suddenly realizes that he has not chosen and will never be able to choose what makes up the very basis for all his actions. For freedom is never given him until after he has been compelled.

In spite of it all, he exists to the full in such an hour of danger. His consciousness is concentrated on this *now* in which his existence is an indisputable fact. Despite it all, he wills and chooses with all his might. Because in his stand to defend his existence he says yes to that will which placed him in this life.

Through the act of choice he displays his primal freedom. And that is the bedrock of every choice he makes. A stand in the face of mortal peril, if taken with the consciousness fully awakened, is a primordial act in the face of that absolute which takes precedence over personal existence and stipulates the condition of it. If a person consciously chooses life, he takes hold, through the fact of existence that has been forced upon him, of the foundation of an imperative which is embodied in the very fact of his being alive, as well as in the flow of his life. In protecting his existence, he will seize the happiness which lies in the total response. That is the happiness of doing the absolutely correct thing at the right moment.

However, we have stated that taking a position in a war of survival means standing on the threshold of faith. This is true because neither an awakened consciousness nor decisiveness of will are things of which one can be automatically assured. They reflect a secret foreknowledge and a mysterious pre-will. In the face of danger, the possibility of rejecting and refusing life also exists. There would then be a dread moment of loss of faith with a gesture of rebellion against the meaningless burden of existence. But this, too, is as rare a possibility as its opposite, because it assumes a belief at its base. In confronting danger, people are usually carried off in a wave that sweeps within and without. They risk their lives as if surrendering themselves to a biological drive. They do it with eyes closed. They act reluctantly, with instinctive fear of facing up in conscious awareness to the situation in which they find themselves. They do not will to will, and they choose not to make a choice.

Only when it is all over does the consciousness awaken, like a refugee hesitantly crawling out of his hiding place and still fearful for his life, and make an affirmation in terms of the emotions of relief and thanksgiving or in terms of panic and humiliation. But most of the time it expresses, in a troubled mixture of relief and humility, the fact that it is still alive. The inner decision to risk life as an obligatory act is a decision to believe. It contains, therefore, a deep mystery. It is an event brought about by something above consciousness and will. It forces men to fight and will, and strengthens them to stand the test.

One does not get such power just from himself. One

can only prepare his heart for it; and the preparation of the heart requires previous education to turn the thoughts and emotions in the direction of the stream of faith. It is quite doubtful whether a person who had not been trained in this manner would be gifted with faith at the moment of mortal fear. It is also doubtful whether he would be able to recognize the threshold over which he was stepping and be able to give it a name. The thrill would pass through such a person like a terribly painful burn in which a latent joy was glowing, without name or title. Beyond it, his decision would be taken as if below the threshold of conscious life. But in the case of the Six-Day War, it appeared that the door had been opened for the mass of Israelis to see, if only vaguely, the essence of the hour.

Why was this so? Because each individual faced the peril as a part of his people. He did so with a sense of belonging to his people and on the basis of identification with his people. The symbols of his national culture, the symbols of a religion by whose power that culture was given a distinctive character, became his personal property.

Jerusalem, the Temple Mount, the Western Wall— all are symbols. That is, they are material objects to which we attach significance. What is the source of that significance? Historical memory. One cannot grasp the symbolic meaning of Jerusalem unless he knows its history.

But even that is not sufficient. A person can have the knowledge and still have nothing happen inside himself when he stands at the Western Wall. Perhaps he will have a sense of frustration: That's it? In order to regain an appreciation of a symbol, a person must come to it in a condition that will make it possible for him to carry away, in a very real sense, the experience which the symbol represents. And that is what happened to a great many Israelis, if only in a dim manner, when Jerusalem was liberated and the first of its liberators stood before the stones of the Western Wall. They had experienced, from within themselves, the same significance which the wall represented outwardly.

It would have been possible, of course, to explain their thrill in a simple and natural way. This was a moment of release from fierce psychological tension. The fear. The exertion. The unbelievable achievement. Was there nothing more than these elements in being present at the Western Wall? No. And—yes. Because the fear and the exertion and the achievement were actualizations of the memory connected with the Western Wall. The symbol was suddenly experienced with direct conscious knowledge of its significance. It therefore gave rise to a sensation of identification with a universal value.

With this we come to the heart of the matter. Direct experience gave the symbol life. But from that moment it was the symbol which gave a name to dumb experience. It made it possible for men to attain the meaning of the sensation they had felt and to experience that sensation with awareness and primal affirmation. Moreover, the symbol gave an interpretation of the sensation on the basis of its reflection in collective experience. That involves more than the experience of the individual. Put it this way: a sensation which one experiences for himself is nameless. It cannot be passed on, and it contains nothing more than its own factuality. But if it happens with another person or a mass of people, it is made transferable and

183

conscious. And with its conscious character it takes on meaning beyond its state of being a mere fact, for it can now be interpreted in terms of a given language and in the context of a certain culture.

Let us go back, for a moment, to our comparison of the War of Independence with the Six-Day War. Standing in the presence of mortal danger gave rise at that time to sensations that were close to religious experience. Anyone who knows the poetry and fiction of the period will find ample support for this judgment. But he can also convince himself that their expression is speechlessly tongue-tied, if he attempts an exhaustive analysis. When they get to the real point, the authors are seized by stammering and thrown into impotence. There was something beyond—but it had no name. The storytellers and poets of the War of Independence did not dare employ religious symbols or the language of the religious experience. Perhaps they never guessed that their experience had been of that type. Can the explanation be that the War of Independence failed to bring about an identification of the individual with the mass that was fighting for survival?

In the War of Independence there was, of course, a sense of identification with a company of fighters. This left a clear imprint upon later literary expression. But that esprit de corps did not foster identification with the entire nation and its history. A sense of belonging to the nation remained at that time an abstraction which never became a personal feeling. The symbols carved from the nation's history and tradition were mere phrases. Individual experience did not fill the void which should have contained the meanings those phrases were meant to express. It was this fact which

184

repelled the honest writer and poet from employing such clichés. The experiences of the literary people therefore remained voiceless.

The Six-Day War was also somewhat different in this respect. This time the company of fighters represented adherence to the nation; we have already discussed the reasons for this change. Early historical conditions and traditional symbols were therefore consciously perceived and fraught with meaning. And, despite the hesitation in doing so, there was no sense of recoil from using them. Thus the private feeling was rescued from inarticulateness, graced with a name, clothed in a symbol, and interpreted. Let us be meticulously specific at this point. Let us not be carried away into describing this sensation as if it were anything more than just the act of setting foot upon the threshold of faith. True inner decision is more than a single moment of dim consciousness. That requires a clear situation. The test of real conviction is not a one-time response, but an answer in terms of an ongoing manner of living.

Like a Penitential Experience

In open confrontation with mortal danger, there is a moment of return to the point of origin. A person relearns the forgotten basic fact of everyday life—that he has been placed in this world and is subject to it. He relearns what is primary and what is secondary, what the end is and what the means. Such an experience demands some reflection, be it ever so hasty. It puts one's whole way of life to the test. With a piercing light it painfully bares one's errors and sins or confirms one's honesty and rightness. Whether he wills it or not, a person passes judgment on his past actions when he is confronted with danger. And his decision, if it is

185

handed down with an awakened consciousness, becomes both a summary of his way of life and a crucial turning point. It is a summary insofar as he extracts a lesson from his personal data. It is a turning point insofar as he determines to correct what he had previously done wrong. It seems to be no exaggeration to state that in the Six-Day War there was a fundamental self-examination, confession of error and guilt, and decision for atonement. The total response to the command had a cleansing value, followed by confession of guilt and the reaffirmation of the original mission, from which we had strayed. There was a renewed orientation after years of neglect.

Self-examination, confession of guilt, act of atonement, purification, reacceptance of mission, and the sense of being under obligation are all the bases of return in the religious sense of the word—penitence. Of course, we would be hyperbolizing if we were to identify the reflective moment of return to the point of origin directly with repentance in its original meaning. If there is no consciousness of being under God's commandment, the word return cannot take on the meaning of repentance. Nevertheless, there is theoretical justification for subsuming these two actions under the same term. Both are return, not only because they are parallel gestures in different spheres, but because there is a qualitative interconnection between these two spheres. This is true insofar as the religious commandment also applies in the social and national spheres of life. We are presented, in this case, with the application of a single form of consciousness in two different spheres of life. Of course, there is a difference between someone who knows the authentic form itself and one who is acquainted with it only in its lower application. However, at the moment of defense of one's existence and of comprehension of the background of one's identification with traditional national-historic symbols, the inner connection is likely to emerge—if only dimly—even in the mind of the man who is not accustomed to think in religious terms. That is, if this was not repentance in the religious sense, it was still a kind of repentance. Or it was on the order of a "shimmer" of repentance.

A Redemptivelike Experience

We may now make our way to the ultimate boundary. We may say that if there was a sort of repentance during the Six-Day War, there was also a sort of salvation. This word, we confess, should be almost unspeakable, much less used in writing. We may employ it only if we have no other term with which to express our intention correctly; and even then we must use it with emphatic reservation, as if simultaneously saying and not saying it. There is no other word like it. None has become so outworn from overuse, a cliché which has lost all meaning. Nevertheless, we need it precisely for the religious connotation it contains, and not for what political Zionism was accustomed to express through it.

Certainly coming back to the land of Israel, even to the entire land of Israel, and even the ingathering of all the exiled Jewish communities in the land are all not redemption in its original sense. That meaning is not present until the gesture of return in the full religious sense is added—the return to faith and Torah. This is even more the case since we are far from the full accomplishment of even the political objective. However, as has been said, our intent is not for such a trite and superficial understanding of the idea of

187

salvation. Nor is our intent for a childish understanding by which redemption is a historic reality that goes beyond the laws of nature and is embodied in myth. These two interpretations are equally far from the mark. Such is the case even though each of them can serve as an external segment of legitimate conceptualizations in theological thought.

The essence of redemption is totality of return in the sense previously described: return to the pristine condition that existed before the first blemish or distortion. Such a time could be depicted as a metahistorical occurrence or even as an event which cancels history out, just as it could also be pictured as a happening within history and in keeping with history's laws. It is described in the Bible in the latter manner. Its symbols are the Sabbath, the sabbatical (seventh) year, and the jubilee year. But there are hours in history when such a reality shines forth on a tangible level, above that of the ritualistic symbol. The fact that the wheel goes back to turning in its accustomed course of faults and errors and failures in no way detracts from the worth of the hour that contains its own purpose. That hour has already been, even though it has no continuation. Such an hour, then, does not solve problems which were not previously solved, nor does it wipe out difficulties which were not overcome beforehand. From this point of view it is the completion of the achievement that had been earlier attained, and nothing more. But it contains an aspect of unexpected grace which cannot be summoned and for which the heart must be prepared.

When history visits a people in an hour of response, it brings lofty uplift and purification. In that hour, difficulties are put out of mind, and the problems which have not been solved are not present, because we are not living with them. So far and no further. Because even such an hour is nothing more than a kind of redemption, but not salvation in its ideal sense. Indeed, history cannot contain an embodiment higher than that. For that reason, we may call the hour of victory in the Six-Day War—in its isolation as an unanticipated summit of the sensation of liberation—an hour of redemption or salvation. The return to the point of origin, in its various aspects, contained a reflection of an ideal pristine condition toward which we aspire but to the essence of which we cannot rise. The strength of faith of one fighting for his life, and the act of identification with the national history and its traditional symbols, both imparted power to this feeling. They endowed it with significance and with a name.

The Six-Day War, then, had a significance that goes far beyond the military and political sphere. That meaning reveals itself if we put our minds, not to the events in and of themselves or to their external interconnections, but to their inner weavings. Indeed, if we turn our attention to the spiritual forces which came to be revealed through these events and to the repeated reaction which they stimulated in the fabric of our feelings and viewpoints, we also can comprehend the religious significance of the war. It witnessed the phenomenon of standing on the threshold of faith. It contained a kind of repentance and a kind of salvation. Something that had been voiceless within us again found expression.

Yet we would err if we were to try to protract the great hour beyond its limit, as if it were a permanent possession. Faith, penitence, and salvation are not achievements to which one clings, but an end for whose realization one struggles. The value of an extraordinary event consists in the opening which it creates for more complete understanding, in the opportunity it offers us. It is up to us whether we shall be able to turn the potentiality into practical reality through education and a radical reconstitution of our lives and thoughts; or whether we shall leave it on the margins of our history as an hour, like other great hours to which we were summoned—but for which we did not have the will to respond.

8

REJOINDER TO TWO OPPONENTS—AN ADDENDUM

Answer To Amos Oz

1. The exalted side that was revealed through the war was, in my opinion, the feeling of love, the devotion to duty, the faith, and the recognition of destiny. These values are diametrically opposite from hate, desire for revenge, and destruction—even when applied to an enemy who attacked us in order to exterminate us. For this reason, I do not know how one can apply this sentence to me: "If the war had not come about through Arab aggression, it would have been proper for us to start it." If we had wanted that war, its experience would have been truly degrading and depressing. Our greatness lay in the fact that we fought as we did in a war which we did not want. I do not ignore the cruel paradox inherent in this fact. But its gravity does not offer sufficient reason to contradict it. We do not desire suffering. We do not desire death. We do not desire war.

But in standing up to suffering, death, and war, man is revealed in his moral greatness, and he fully learns what is inside him. It is no crime to recognize this and say it. Admittedly, tests of this kind are not sweet melodramas. They are moments of terrifying mortal dread. I do not hide from that fact. It is for that reason that I have pointed out that one who is fighting for

survival stands at a threshold on which he can acquire
—or lose—faith. One may sense the marvelous within
the terror, or grasp only the terror itself and be cast
down. What determines the choice between these
two possibilities? That is a matter for the heart of the
individual. But let me be permitted to note that the
difference between them is dialectic and that they are
juxtaposed over against one another. The experience
of Amos Oz in the war, therefore, is no further from
my own experience than seems right to him. When all
is said and done, the protest which he voices against
the injustice and degradation of war is not exactly the
stand of a degraded man.

2. Amos Oz is not being precise when he states that
I ignored the Arabs in my essay. They are present in
my writing—as an enemy, in a simple and literal
sense. They are a cruel and unrelenting enemy who
renewed the terror of the Holocaust for us and forced
us to see our historic destiny in its tragic uniqueness.
We did not cause that. It was the foe who compelled
us to face up to him precisely at that level. It therefore
seems quite human that before and during the war I
did not keep an account of his sufferings and rights. At
that time, my mind was not at all free for such things.
It was for that reason that the joy over the victory
seemed simply justified to me. That joy was beclouded
by nothing except the sorrow over those of our sol-
diers who fell.

We were saved and relieved. The possibility of exer-
cising our rights over our homeland—a possibility
which the Arabs had intransigently denied us—was
opened for us. (And the exercise of those rights does
not necessarily mean denying the rights of the Arabs.)
In this regard it is fitting to admit that it was the

victory which liberated us from feelings of hatred toward the enemy. It was only the victory which allowed us to see the Arabs, after the war, as Amos Oz
sees them. May I be allowed to state the way I try to
see them, although after the emotional shock it is no
easier for me to see them this way than for the Arabs
to take the same view of me? I would like to regard
them as human beings for whose sufferings one must
feel, to honor their rights and to search for a just solution along with them. It goes without saying that this
problem must be faced in the proper context. I find
nothing in the concept of a "time of return" which
contradicts this. For it seems to me that my statements
stand the test of the moral values that obligate me as
both man and Jew.

Reply To Pinchas Rosenblüth

First, let me emphasize a distinction about which I
wanted to be careful in my essay, though apparently
I was unsuccessful in this respect. There is a difference
between an analysis of the causes of a great spiritual
event, in contradistinction to the specification that
those causes are good and desirable in and of themselves. In "A Time of Returning," I proceeded from
the assumption—one which seems not to be alien
even to P. Rosenblüth—that something great happened in the Six-Day War, from the spiritual point of
view as well as from the military and political standpoint. I asked myself what it was that had happened,
and why it happened. What was the essence of the
experience, and what was its background? I made no
judgment on the value of the political outcome, nor
did it ever occur to me to impart a religious significance to it, as Rosenblüth asserted in his letter. Politi-

cal and military realities must be evaluated in political and military terms. One who is not privy to the secrets of Providence surely has no way of endowing them with religious significance. From the viewpoint of my study in "A Time of Returning," the battlefield was important as the condition in which the inner spiritual event occurred, and I dealt with it solely in this respect.

Now, in order to remove all doubt, let me say this: I never thought, nor do I now think, that we could rightfully go to war solely in order to expand our borders over the entirety of our homeland—even though I believe in our historic right over it. I surely do not consider as errors our acceptance of the partition plan or our unwillingness to start a war for the liberation of Jerusalem on our own initiative with an aggressive act. Moreover, I see no necessary connection between what I wrote in "A Time of Returning" and the ideas of the movement for retention of the whole of the land of Israel. For myself, I do not reject the idea of partial withdrawal and compromise, if they assure peace. (Peace, if it is true peace, will have to guarantee us the right to live in those parts of our homeland which are not under Jewish control, just as the Arabs might live in those parts of their homeland which are not under Arab control.)

War is one of the worst things that mankind can bring upon itself. There should be no resort to war unless no other choice remains for protecting life and independence. Therefore, if we had started a war with the Arabs in order to expand our hold over the land of Israel and to deprive the Arabs of their rights, that would have been an act devoid of moral justification. It could not have fostered that psychological thrill or that spiritual introspection. It was only because war was forced upon us as a necessary means of defending our rights, and not on the basis of hatred of the enemy, that the liberation of the Old City of Jerusalem took on such significance for both the religious group and the secularists. It was only in this manner that a stone wall—the liberation of which for its own sake would not be worth a single drop of blood—became the symbol of the resurrection of a nation after its destruction and subsequent return to its life-giving homeland. I therefore accept Rosenblüth's words on this subject to the effect that war never was and does not now have to be regarded as a means to the fulfillment of Zionism. The Zionist way was and must always be the way of peaceful settlement.

But we cannot ignore the fact that our hope that the Arabs would understand us and make their peace with us and with our vision of restoration has not been fulfilled. Their violent opposition prevented us from realizing the original concept of Zionism. The accomplishment we achieved with the establishment of the State had to be made secure through war. After the war, the hostility which closed in on us threatened to destroy us. Throughout the first nineteen years of the existence of the State of Israel, we saw no chance of changing this reality. We led our lives in an atmosphere of frustration. This, in my opinion, was the main cause of the decline in public morality. Willingness to do pioneering work waned, and its place was appropriated by a mania for enjoyment of the tiny gain that had been made. Sadly, it was not possible to alter our external circumstances without repeated warfare. That was forced upon us by mounting and thoroughgoing hostility. We had no desire for war, nor do we want it now. But no choice was left us, and we fought, and the ring of siege was broken. Since the latent moral strength of the people reappeared through war and the nation arrived at a consciousness of its own worth, is it then a sin to look upon what was brought about by the war as a liberating event? Is that not the plain truth?

To return to the question of the results of the war, the facts are surely with Rosenblüth in his statement that we are far from a solution and that we confront serious problems and terrible dangers both from within and without. It is even possible that they will force us to withdraw without achieving peace, and that the opportunity presented us will be no more. In "A Time of Returning" I never claimed that the "original concept of Zionism has been realized." I wrote that we had been given a chance to fulfill it and that the matter was in our own hands. From this standpoint, we have had an experience of turning from a frustration that broke our will and our sense of obligation, to a hope that invests us with willpower and duty. Was not that estimate correct? Is it not also correct now that we have encountered the whole complex of difficult problems which have come into being with the new situation—indeed, is it not correct because of them?

The case is the same in regard to what I have written about the renewal of recognition of the unique character of the Jewish people among the nations. Rosenblüth is right in stating that being persecuted does not mean being special or chosen. What I wrote described only the cause which brought many of us back once again to see the fate of the Jewish people within the total fabric of its history and to grasp, on this basis, the meaning of our cultural heritage. It goes without saying that the awareness of that special character can take on meaning only on the basis of that spiritual heritage, not from the mere facts of tragic isolation and fear of extermination. That is, only when we saw ourselves isolated and on the brink of destruction—because we were Jews and because of the special burden and the unique role of Jewry in the world—could the consciousness of our uniqueness and our election awaken again among us. And did not that awareness stir among us at that time?

Now I come to the main problem, one which appears to contain the fundamental difference between my views and those of Rosenblüth. Was there a religious dimension to the war experience? Again I stress that in my statements about a religious dimension I did not mean the war itself, nor was I referring to its immediate results. I did not regard the victory itself as a miracle, nor the mere conquest of the country as the redemption. The miraculous element that was revealed was embodied in the power of faith, and the liberation of the country is nothing more than an opportunity that can be made into actuality by settlement and striving for peace. For this reason, I was particularly careful in "A Time of Returning" to speak of the religious significance of the experience of war and victory and not of the meaning of the war and the victory themselves. Indeed, I am of the opinion that this experience had a religious significance. It seems to me that the difference between my view and that of Rosenblüth lies mainly in our understanding of the tie between the sphere of life of the believer and the customary sphere of life of the "secular" man. Is there a connection between them, or are they two planes between which there is no contact?

From Rosenblüth's words, one gathers that there is

a sharp gap between the two planes. My own statements are meant to assert that faith is anchored in the
sphere of experience of every man, like a flame flicker-
ing over the coals. Of course, only an education based
on religious tradition can cause the flicker to burst into
a permanently light-giving flame. One who is cut off
from the continuity of tradition, therefore, knows a
lack of faith. At times, he is not conscious of the lack.
But at any rate it is clear to him that he does not stand
in encounter with the explicit command of revelation;
he is not in the presence of God.

Nevertheless, it seems to me that in moments of
extreme trial, in times of great suffering or great happiness, when a person confronts the fact of his having
been placed in the world and the fact of his freedom
to choose or reject life, he stands on the verge of the
absolute as at a threshold where he can gain or lose
faith. And if he has this experience, not in isolation,
but together with a mass of people and against the
background of the heritage of that people, he is likely
to recognize the condition in which he exists in terms
of that tradition. That is, he may rediscover the en-
trance to the tradition from which he has been cut off.
I was referring to this experience in "A Time of Returning." Be that as it may, it seems to me that such
was the meaning of the spiritual event which occurred
during the Six-Day War. Against that background, I
described that experience as a sort of penitential return and a sort of salvation in the inner sense, as a
totality of return. A *sort* of salvation and a *sort* of
repentance, because I regarded the entire matter as
a beginning which could be used as a base, and nothing more. It follows that I am in emphatic agreement
with Rosenblüth's reservations when he avers that the

test of faith is not the momentary sensation, no matter how great that it, but the ongoing course of daily life. Indeed, there is no assurance that the experience we shared will really lead many people to build their lives on its foundation. The reality we achieved does not offer perfection, and there is great danger in identifying it with the redemption. And, of course, the letdown we encountered after the War of Independence may be lying in wait for us after this war, too. Rosenblüth is right when he says that the true change can occur only through inner education and elevation. Is it not clear that I did not come to preach war as a liberating experience or to advocate self-fortification in the results of war as if it were the final redemption? Is it not plain that my intent was to make a contribution to that effort in behalf of inner education and elevation? It now appears to be stated in so many words.

9
ISRAEL
AND THE JEWS OF THE DIASPORA

I

In the following, I shall discuss only one of the many phases of the subject at hand: What must and what can the State of Israel be for the Jewish people? What must and what can it give to Jewry? On what basis has it the right to impose demands on the Jewish people? These are questions which occupy us unceasingly after the Six-Day War. And the changes wrought in Israel and abroad by that war have made these questions all the more serious.

The State, as the great achievement of the Zionist movement, was created on the assumption that it would offer the total solution to both the Jewish question and the question of Judaism in modern times. But the difficulties in the path of realizing this solution were obvious from the start. The doubts as to whether it would be possible to assemble the entire Jewish people or the largest part of it in the land of Israel accompanied Zionist thinkers and leaders constantly. But those who laid the foundations of the new Jewish community in Palestine did their work, for the most part, with the conviction that it was an imperative matter. And since it was imperative, it was also possible, despite the gigantic obstacles that stood in the way.

201

It is true that, until the establishment of the State, the Zionist movement was marked by a paradoxical tension between the presence and absence of extreme realism. There was thorough realism in the willingness to look upon present distresses with open eyes and to see clearly the future terrors that lay in wait for Diaspora Jewry. But there was a lack of ultimate realism in Zionism's willingness to work for the accomplishment of its vision in spite of the fact that the political, social, and economic chances for it were quite slim. Let us confess that if that vision was achieved—even partially—it came about more than a little because of the devotion and perseverance which flowed out of a consciousness of the ruin that could be expected to come upon the Diaspora, as well as from the almost irrational hope of gaining a complete success in Palestine.

Be that as it may, within the framework of an ideology that was demanding a total solution, the question of what Israel should be for Jewry could be rather simply, clearly, and briefly answered. It would have to be everything that a normal state can be for a normal people. It would be a homeland in which the great majority of Jews would gather. It would offer a structure of political independence that would assure the survival and well-being of the people. It would enable the Jews to build a healthy and well-ordered society in which the Hebrew language would flourish and Jewish culture would bloom. Such an entity would not be possible except in Palestine. Thus the existence of the Diaspora was only a thing of the moment, only an anticipation of the people's assembling in their independent state. The Exile had no set mold other than the structure of the Zionist movement, which was organizing the nation for the rebuilding of its state. Such a framework provided that Jewish communities might continue to exist in the Diaspora only insofar as they banded together in working for the establishment of the Jewish state, and even then only on the condition that they move to it when it was created.

II

Faith in that solution, which I intentionally formulated somewhat simplistically and schematically, eroded, as we know, with the establishment of the State. As I have said, I doubt whether Zionism could have achieved its partial, though decisive, success if the Zionist movement had not set its sights on a total achievement. But once the partial accomplishment had taken place, the weight of various factors underwent a reversal of evaluation in the Zionist movement's considerations. The movement became more soberly realistic in estimating the chances for total realization of political, social, and economic goals. And it became unrealistic in respect to its sensitivity toward dangers threatening the Jewish communities abroad on every hand. During the first nineteen years of the State's existence, the feeling grew stronger and stronger, though it was difficult to formulate it explicitly, that the partial accomplishment was also the maximum attainable; furthermore, even that accomplishment was very hard to sustain in full. For this purpose it was thought necessary to mobilize the supreme efforts of the Jewish people. Why? First, because of Israel's narrow borders. We saw no chance of expanding them in the face of the Arab states' hostility. And second, because of the few prospects for large-scale immigration from either the countries of eastern Europe or the affluent lands.

It became clear that the process of normalization after the Holocaust had rather easily achieved marked success in, of all places, certain parts of the Diaspora. It even appeared that the Jews had no need of the State of Israel in the sense of a homeland to which one would come in order to rebuild. For the most part, they had no desire to live in it. And it was doubtful that they had need of it in the process of striking roots in the economic, political, social, and cultural life of Europe and America. Mounting hostility and growing indifference pressed in from opposite sides. Together they caused the citizens of the State and the members of the Zionist movement to reconcile themselves to the diminished image of Zionism's original vision. The State of Israel would take its place as one Jewish center alongside other such centers. It would be a center with a certain special quality and perhaps also a special function. But nothing more than that.

How was the answer to our question worded in this situation? What *could* the State of Israel be for the Jews of the Diaspora? During Israel's first nineteen years, there was a more and more powerful tendency to adopt Ahad Ha-am's idea of the spiritual center as a substitute for the original program of Zionism. The State of Israel could be a focus of national pride for all Jews. For them, it could be a center of authentic Jewish culture. This could include literature, art, science, scholarship, and perhaps also folklore. Torah would go forth from this center to the rest of the Jewish communities. They would depend upon the center in their confrontation with European and American culture, the attraction of which might assimilate and submerge them.

Was there anything to this solution? It appears to me that we can reply to that question, without much heartache, in the absolute negative. The State of Israel was not and could never have been made into such a spiritual center. In principle it must be set forth that no individual or community ever takes part in a culture in a passive manner, as if receiving a gift from someone else. Participation in a culture means active involvement in the process of creativity. For this reason, a Jewish group which has no active focus of Jewish community life or independent Jewish creative culture of its own can never take part in the cultural creativity of another Jewish center.

At the very most a Diaspora Jew might pick out some colorful aspects of an exotic way of life for himself along with some bits of marginal culture. These might serve as a plaything for the young and offer a little nostalgia to the senior citizens. But such things would and could give people nothing with which to stand up against the influence of a culture within which they were actually creating living values. The superficiality of Jewish culture among the vast majority of the Jews of Europe and America is irrefutable proof of the validity of this assertion. Ahad Ha-am's concept of a spiritual center was, from this point of view, devoid of all substance from the beginning.

But suppose it was possible to delineate the life of Diaspora Jewry as a periphery around about an Israeli center. Could that center raise itself to the level of Jewish cultural creativity imparted to it by such a role assignment? On this, too, I am inclined to respond in the negative. Once again we are face to face with an astonishing paradox. In the years preceding the establishment of the State, the Jewish community in Palestine served, in practice, as a spiritual center for a large part of Diaspora Jewry—despite the fact that the overwhelming majority of the Yishuv tended to reject Ahad Ha-am's idea. In what way was this so? Because the Jewish community in Palestine was a creative focus for the Jews of the world, or at least for those Jews whose considerations dwelt on the work of Zionist realization. They regarded the Palestinian pioneer as their emissary, and the halutz looked upon himself in exactly the same way. They lived their lives as Jews oriented to Palestine, even if they did not fulfill the obligation of *aliyah*.

After the establishment of the State, when the concept of a spiritual center gained wide acceptance, the idea lost that significance. This happened because the direct tie between the Zionist movement and its work was severed. It was no longer possible to regard the land of Israel as a direct project for Diaspora Jewry. The land of Israel began to lead a life on its own along separate political and social lines. It ceased to represent the dispersed Jewish people. Although Israel began building its economy and society along with the other Jewish centers, it did not do so with their purposes in mind. Israel, of course, had a uniqueness as an independent Jewish center from the political point of view. But it still did not become the political state for the entire Jewish people. This being the case, the Jewish community in Israel stopped regarding itself and living as a Zionist Yishuv. That is, it ceased to see its work of settlement in the land of Israel as having significance for the destiny of the whole Jewish people.

The above refers particularly to the young generation born in Palestine. For them, the act of living in Eretz Israel never had some higher meaning, nor did they ever experience any Jewish value through it. They might cling to their country, but they would do so like members of any other people. And like all the others they might also leave it through emigration if presented with some captivating inducement; in this, too, they would never feel as if they were betraying their people. Zionism thus achieved its ambition for the normalization of Jewish life in Israel. But paradoxically it had to face the fact that this longed-for process of normalization itself posed a danger for the Zionist movement's work.

Indisputably, a Jew living a "normal" life in Israel without having to struggle with the problem of his own unique Jewish identity—because this is apparently assured by the existing social and political structure—has lost something. He has lost his attachment to the Jewish people. And he has also lost his attachment to the unique culture of the Jewish people. That is, he has undergone a process of assimilation into European culture.

The reality in Israel seems to bear out this judgment through many aspects of life. The Jewish people has been subject, in Israel and the Diaspora, to parallel processes of normalization, though under differing political and social circumstances. And this fact has enlarged the gap between Israel and the Diaspora. But has not Israel at least maintained a superiority from the point of view of aspiration to normalization? To a definite extent, Israel has maintained such advantage. For even in the affluent, comfortable countries, the Jews are far from the complete social rootedness of which they boast. However, in a different sense, life in a tiny state offering meager opportunities and surrounded by hate does not permit one to take root either. Nor does it foster involvement in the creativity of that European culture to which we have aspired and still do aspire. From this point of view, the Jews of Europe and the United States have been closer to the center, while it is we who have been the ones on the periphery, feeling that we are not accomplishing anything.

The conclusion is simple. To the extent that our cultural orientation has been determined by a desire to be like other nations, the unique Jewish content in our creativity has decreased. The idea that we should be a spiritual center for Jewish groups that are richly rooted in the culture of their environment appears to be a curious and ridiculous conceit. From this point of view, we are deriving more nourishment from them than they ever could from us. Only by the creation of Jewish culture can we surpass them and perhaps give them help. But that would require a thoroughgoing change in orientation.

At any rate, according to the line of thought that has evolved in the life of the Israeli Jewish community since the establishment of the State, it is clear that the concept of a spiritual center has no basis. This is the case because the power of Israeli Jewry to bring into being a unique and independent cultural creation has diminished, just as has the ability of the Diaspora to take a creative part in such a culture. This, in my opinion, is one of the main causes of the confused groping which has afflicted the Zionist movement since the establishment of Israel. And this is also one of the principal factors in the feeling of frustration and confusion which reached its peak and its anxiety-producing acme on the eve of the Six-Day War.

III

The Six-Day War marked a profound turning point. First, our evaluation of the political potentialities was altered. The earlier partial achievement could no longer be looked upon as a maximum gain. Understandably, we had to free ourselves from the stunning effect of our accomplishment on the battlefield. A military victory does not guarantee the opportunity it makes possible. It must be followed by a political and demographic victory, and such gains were not guaranteed to us. But the opportunity was created; and to a great extent it was up to us as to whether that opportunity should be seized or missed. A change took place in the spiritual orientation of the Jewish community in Israel. Identification with the Jewish people was strengthened. Identification with Jewish history also became more powerful. And the act of living in the land of Israel once again became charged with that high significance it had possessed in the pre-State period. In this sense, the Israeli Jew became a Zionist.

Perhaps a change also occurred in the spiritual life of Diaspora Jewry, though this is a topic on which we must be most cautious. The fact that the Jews of America responded as they did to the danger that threatened Israel is evidence of their feelings of rootedness in the social and political life of the United States no less than of their identification with the State of Israel. This is demonstrated by the fact that they were far from daring to respond in a similar fashion during the Holocaust. Only now have they felt themselves strong enough to identify forcefully with their brothers—because only now do they feel that they are Americans in the full sense of the word. It therefore required a large measure of naiveté to believe that there would be a wave of immigration to Israel from the free world after the war. However, it seems that something shifted even in this regard.

All of this brought about—with some justification— a process of recapitulation in Zionist thought. Nonetheless, it seems to me that we would be committing a gross error if we regarded this change as a victory for Zionism in terms of the Zionist movement's classic formulations. What was made clear with certainty during the State's nineteen years preceding the war is still valid. We must learn to grasp the meaning of the matter from the standpoint of the question of the place of Israel in the life of the Jewish people. First, classic Zionism made the assumption that the Jewish people was threatened with *physical destruction* because of the anti-Semitism that was rooted in European culture. It was therefore necessary to establish a Jewish state to serve as a place of safe refuge. This was also to bring about a normalization of Jewish life by the reduction of the tension between Jewry and its environment.

This assumption has not been confirmed in its entirety and in its simplistic form by recent and current events. I shall not enter into a discussion of whether the position of Jewry in the democratic countries is as solid as most of its representatives claim. I assume that their evaluation is rather optimistic and that it frequently proceeds from an ignoring of facts which they find unwelcome. But that is not the subject we are discussing. The issue I want to stress now is that during all the years of the existence of the State of Israel it has become clear in practice—and this received quite dramatic confirmation during the Six-Day War—that the tragic conflict between Jew and Gentile is no longer

focused on the Diaspora but on the relationship between the State of Israel and its neighbors. In this area,
the tension between Jewry and the nations of the
world has increased in every respect. This is the case
from the national-political point of view. It applies to
our relations with the Arabs and, through them, with
all the powers concerned with the Middle East.

It also applies from the spiritual-religious point of
view. In this respect, it suffices to emphasize that
Christianity has still not reconciled itself to the creation of a Jewish state in the Holy Land. For Christians,
this is quite a grave theological and political question.
And it is certain that Islam has not made its peace with
the reality of Israel, particularly in regard to Jerusalem. Moreover, we have brought all this tension to a
higher pitch through the establishment of the State.
We have created a state in surroundings which were
not prepared to accept that state peaceably, and in a
world whose attitude toward it was ambivalent, to say
the least. And we must go back and struggle for our
very survival and for the justification of our existence
in our own country.

I wish to stress at this point that the core of peril
revealed in Israel is a threat to the entire Jewish people, not just to the Jewish community in Palestine.
This is because the hostility against Israel expressed—
directly or indirectly—the attitude toward the Jewish
people as such, and insofar as Jewry stands guard over
its independence and its special character.

Indeed, this connection stands out from two points
of view. First, we have become convinced that the
attitude of governments and peoples toward the State
of Israel has had an influence directly upon their relationship with the Jews living among them. To mention

only one example, the gravity of the danger imperiling the Jews in the Arab countries is a direct result of the conflict between those lands and Israel. This fact has come to appear natural and self-explanatory to us. But even the situation of the Jews of eastern Europe, especially the Soviet Union and Poland, reflects the relationship of those governments to the State of Israel. And during the recent war, it became clear that the Jewry of a West European country like France could also suffer a deterioration in position because of its government's relationship to Israel.

Further, the existence of Israel puts a heavy burden upon the change in Christian attitudes toward the Jewish people in large sections of the church. It is not impossible that a condition might be created whereby identification with the State of Israel might place even a deep-rooted and self-confident Jewry such as that of the United States in quite an unpleasant dilemma. If the interests of the United States should happen to conflict substantially with those of the State of Israel, the problem could become one of great gravity. Indeed, it is reasonable to assume that at the heart of these questions latent anti-Semitism is at work. Its source is religious-cultural or social. It is an anti-Semitism which has not waned and will not do so in the near future, in either the truly progressive countries or in those which call themselves progressive. That is why we have said that it is the attitude toward Israel which focuses these peoples' attitude to the Jew as such. The relationship to Israel is what rouses anti-Semitism out of a latent state and sets it ablaze. Attitudes toward the State of Israel are what give anti-Semitism its ideological lines in our age.

Here is an instructive phenomenon. Instead of Jew-hatred based on religious ideology (as in the Middle Ages), or anti-Semitism founded upon racial ideology (as at the beginning of the modern age), today animosity against the Jews—especially in countries where racial or religious discrimination is to be ruled out—is based upon political ideology in the form of anti-Zionism.

This is not surprising. For it is the relationship to the State of Israel which expresses and symbolizes the separateness of the Jew from his surroundings. That is what marks him as different, as foreign. If he were to renounce his tie to the State of Israel and renounce altogether and for all practical purposes his tie to Jewishness, such a renunciation would certainly dissipate his environment's aggressive attitude toward him.

With this, we come to the second aspect of the question. During the Six-Day War it became clear, even to those who refused to admit the fact, that the survival of the State of Israel was vital for the survival of Diaspora Jewry. For if the State did not survive, they would not long be able to preserve their Jewish identification. They would be assimilated to the degree permitted by their environment. This, in my judgment, accounts for the astonishing devotion shown by American Jewry to Israeli interests. This was certainly not caused by anxiety for the American Jew's own political fate. (On the contrary, the self-assurance of United States Jewry enabled it to respond as it did.) Rather, it suddenly became plain to all that American Jewry could not permit a situation in which Israel would be left open to her enemies. American Jewry's responsibility for Israel was the supreme test of its loyalty to itself.

This, then, is the rationale by which we may and

must demand the immigration of Jews from the countries of the free world to Israel in order to assure the survival of the State, its peace and integrity, and its Jewish character. This is not a manifestation of populational interests. The State of Israel focuses its struggle on the continuation of the existence and the special nature of the Jewish people. The State may even impose the obligation of immigration in the name of the entire Jewish people's will to survive and create.

It would seem, however, that it is no longer legitimate to represent the demand for immigration as an aspiration for normalization in the economic or political sense. In those respects, the Jew can find easier remedy in the democratic countries. He can attain a physical security much greater than the State of Israel is able to offer him at present. But he can win all this only at the cost of forgoing or endangering his own Jewish identity or that of his descendants. When we fight for the preservation of Jewish identity in the Diaspora, we are actually struggling against this process of normalization. When all is said and done, we are worsening the condition of Jewish communities. Without the State of Israel they would, perhaps, gradually assimilate and be absorbed into their environment. But we, knowingly and willfully, demand that Jews living in countries where they enjoy a comfortable situation take quite a tense spiritual and intellectual stand vis-à-vis their surroundings. For the preservation of Jewish identification implies an attitude of separateness within openness to the environment in order to avoid the peril of assimilation. And assimilation is the natural derivative of thoroughgoing normalization.

IV

Against this background we must answer the question of what Israel can and should be for the Jews of the Diaspora. Let me first sum up what it *cannot* be. The State of Israel cannot describe itself as the sole secure refuge from the danger of destruction or persecution. Those Jews who are suffering—who are behind the iron curtain—are unable to come to Israel. Jewry which *can* come is in no danger. Also, it is doubtful whether the State of Israel can be called a "safe refuge." It is an embattled fortress, a stronghold that has to be continually strengthened. For this need, too, we are demanding immigration.

Nor can Israel serve as a spiritual center in the Ahad Ha-am sense of the term. For, as we have said, this is not the way a culture is created. And this is not the way in which one participates in a culture. True, Israel can function as a focus of identification with Judaism and the Jewish people, as we learned during the Six-Day War. It can be a guarantee for the continued existence of the Jewish people. But if we wish Israel to fulfill an ongoing role, and not just be satisfied with the arousing of nationalistic sentiments in times of crisis, then it is imperative that the State of Israel stand at the center of Jewish activity directed toward the State itself. Educational work, social activity, and cultural projects, as well as economic works—with all of which immigration to Israel and life in Israel stand in a tension of realization and creativity—are the supreme test.

This means a renewal of Zionism as a movement giving utterance to the active tie between Israel and the Diaspora. It means the conversion of Zionism into the principle instrument of connection between the

State and Jewry abroad. Today we have no delusions that a mass immigration would ensue and concentrate most of the Jewish people in its homeland. We have also dispelled the fierce vision which predicted that Jewish survival outside of Israel would be impossible. We are only arguing that a Jewry which is not in a process of alienation from itself and is not drifting away from its origins, a Jewry which is striving to base itself on its true sources and to embrace its own genuine values, will find the most consistent expression of its Jewish loyalty in *aliyah.*

Immigration is, therefore, for Diaspora Jews—especially for the young—the supreme test of their loyalty to themselves. *Aliyah* is both the symbol and the guarantee of the continuation of the living tie between all Jews everywhere and the State of Israel. It is through immigration to Israel that the connection among all segments of world Jewry is secured.

The Zionist movement which educates for *aliyah* as the test of fulfillment for its own values can tie the rest of the sections of the Jewish community to intensive Jewish activity and to participation—in various degrees of intensiveness—in the life of the State through settlement, social construction, and cultural creativity. For a Diaspora which has a part in the upbuilding of the State, Israel is a focus of identification and a true spiritual center.

One might ask what compensation Israel can provide a Jew who gives up all the advantages of life in an affluent country in order to come and build. What can Israel offer the Jew who places himself in the complex of dual loyalty in the land of his residence? The simplest reply is that Israel can give him nothing except the opportunity to give himself what he owes himself. Israel makes it possible for him to be a Jew in his actions and his creativity. No more, no less.

It goes without saying that everything possible must be done to ease the absorption of Jews from the free world, both socially and economically. But it seems to me that it is a mistake—and a most grave one—if we represent such concessions as a solution of the problem of immigration, as if the guarantee of nice conditions is enough to attract *aliyah*. Immigration can be attracted. You do not attract *aliyah;* you demand it as a matter of national response. And the condition without which we shall have no right to demand *aliyah* is that we open the door for the newcomer to participate actively and consciously in the creation of Jewish life in the State of Israel. He must be able to work, feeling that he is giving his best, that he is fulfilling his humanity, and that he is making a tangible contribution to the Israeli Jewish community. In sum, he must sense that there is importance and value in his living in Israel.

The question, then, is one of updating the structures of Zionist work: settlement in the land and what follows that act. It appears to me that on this subject we must return to what the pioneers of the second and third *aliyah*s have to teach us: if a person comes to the land of Israel, or is already living in it, with the thought of getting "what's coming to him," he will get very little out of it. He will receive much less than he would be able to obtain in many other places around the world. Israel is poor, and the opportunities it offers are limited. Even if we improve the conditions of absorption to the peak of our powers, a person attracted to Israel in this manner is bound to be disappointed. But if he comes to Israel out of a desire to measure up, to create, to contribute to his people, he will, as a Jew, obtain infinitely more that he could find anywhere else in the world. In creating, he will find himself.

V

It goes without saying that the foregoing also applies to those who already live in Israel. During the nineteen years of the State preceding the Six-Day War, we learned that even in Israel it is possible to live as one does in the Diaspora. We have been made aware that there is always a difference between a life in Israel that is lived on the basis of a full emotion-ideological commitment—expressing itself in a willingness for deeds—and an undistinguished life lived in Israel because of circumstances of fate that have not been reflectively and consciously chosen. And there is an eternal difference between living in Israel with a spiritual orientation of need and doing so on the basis of commitment. However, such statements are beyond the scope of our present discussion.

It is my wish, finally, to make note of a way of understanding the function of the State as an entity that lays down a challenge and bears a demand that impels even the State itself—that is, even its institutions and leadership—toward a certain orientation.

First and foremost, the institutions and leadership should not be self-centered or devoted to their own particularistic interests. Rather, they should keep in mind their duty and responsibility to the entire Jewish people. Identification with the State must have the meaning of identification with the entire people, not just satisfaction of the interests of a part of the Jewish people.

These words would appear to be obvious. They need no special emphasis. But is the theory observed in practice? I doubt very much if it is. Take one example. For the Zionist movement truly to be a working bridge between the Diaspora and Israel, it must be constructed as a people's movement. That implies before anything else that the movement be structured upon a substantial social base, on a Zionist group that elects its own leadership and guides the leadership's activity in keeping with the group's views, after proper discussion and debate. Is this the situation today? Are the political parties prepared to renounce their power over the institutions of the Zionist movement and give way to the leadership of the movement itself? The last Zionist Congress was far from giving an encouraging answer to this question.* From this point of view, it stirred up an unacceptable picture in the mind of anyone who was expecting a real change.

Or take another example. So that the Jewish people abroad can become a partner in the life of the State by means of the Zionist movement, the State must genuinely involve the Zionist leadership in many of the areas of Israel's activities. To involve the movement means to listen to its opinion, to give it consideration, and to share executive authority with it. Has such willingness been apparent in government discussions on this problem? Only to a slight degree, it seems to me, and even that without much enthusiasm.

Let us take still another example. We would want identification with Israel to be truly an identification with the Jewish people and with all that is most dear to it. But in order to bring this about, Israel must not

---

* *The reference is to the 27th Zionist Congress. Encouraging progress was made at the 28th Zionist Congress, yet it is still not satisfactory.*

keep in mind only its own welfare. It must not simply represent the interests of that group of Jews gathered within the State. It must also represent a responsibility for the unity and peace of the entire Jewish people, even if that does not seem to serve some particular Israeli interest.

But does the State of Israel always conduct itself that way? Israel managed the struggle for a change in attitude on the part of the authorities of the Soviet Union toward Soviet Jews in a hesitant manner. The fate of Soviet Jewry was hardly mentioned at the 27th Zionist Congress. And on international platforms, Israel consistently refrained from raising the question in its full form.* This arouses one's suspicions that considerations of some particularistic Israeli political application, real or imaginary, may have been given precedence over the weight of obligation and responsibility for Jewry as a whole. As long as the State acts in this fashion, it has no chance of becoming, in practice and at all times, the focus of identification with the Jewish people.

Let me sum up these matters in a brief statement. The Six-Day War brought us back to a starting point on which much that expresses our devotion to an ideal depends. Whether the State of Israel can become a center of Jewish activity and identification depends not only on external circumstances, but upon us. We may let the historical moment slip by; we may go back to existing as a peripheral Jewish community. We can

---

* Such was the situation in 1968. Now a deep change has occurred under the impact of the tremendous activity of Russian Jews and that of olim from Russia in Israel. Still I believe that the possibility of a particularistic Israeli policy is best shown in this instance. We should be aware of this possibility and stand guard.

be one among the rest of the Jewish communities in the countries of the world. Each of them is busy with its own concerns. And each of them is continually growing more and more alienated from the others and from its own Jewish identification.

It is for us to make the choice between these alternatives.

98239